The Long Struggle

The Muslim World's Western Problem

The Long Struggle

The Muslim World's Western Problem

Amil Khan

Winchester, UK
Washington, USA

First published by Zero Books, 2010
Zero Books is an imprint of John Hunt Publishing Ltd., The Bothy, Deershot Lodge, Park Lane, Ropley, Hants, SO24 0BE, UK
office1@o-books.net
www.zero-books.net

For distributor details and how to order please visit the 'Ordering' section on our website.

ISBN: 978 1 84694 368 3

A CIP catalogue record for this book is available from the British Library.

Design: Stuart Davies

Printed in the UK by CPI Antony Rowe
Printed in the USA by Offset Paperback Mfrs, Inc

CONTENTS

Introduction

The first Jihadi fighter I ever met had a serious crush on Lebanese singer Nancy Ajram. We were sitting in a café in Cairo as George W. Bush and Tony Blair prepared to invade Iraq, and although Hisham was supposed to be telling me why he was ready to die in Iraq, he couldn't take his eyes off Nancy sashaying on the screen behind us as she breathily sang; "I'll torment you, but I won't leave you."

After two years freelancing in the Middle East, I joined Reuters in Cairo in early 2003. America was preparing to lead its allies in an invasion of Iraq that the world's Muslims thought was part of a Western grand plan to steal oil and protect Israel. In my first few weeks, I had proved absolutely useless at the basic Reuters skills of writing reports quickly and without factual or typographical errors. In an effort to prove to my boss that employing me really was a good idea, I decided to show her that although I might mix up prices and percentages on a stock market report, I could get a good story.

I'd heard rumors that a steady stream of young Egyptians were travelling to Iraq to fight the invasion, but no one I knew could arrange a meeting. I spent day after day trying to charm activists from left-wing political parties and the banned Islamist Muslim Brotherhood. When I had run out of ideas, I found the men I was looking for literally on my doorstep. The Iraqi embassy was opposite my flat. I had seen an unusually large number of men outside it every day for weeks. It finally occurred to me that they might be trying to get to Iraq.

I walked towards a group of men standing outside the small darkened doors of the large white building newly adorned with pictures of Saddam Hussein, but stopped as I drew close. While I was standing on the kerb thinking of something to say, one of the younger men came over to me and said; "Are you Iraqi?"

I said that I wasn't, but didn't want to give away my British nationality in case the group decided not to like me on the spot. Instead, I resorted to my parents' original nationality and said I was Pakistani.

"So, you want to get to Iraq too," he guessed.

Before I could even begin to unravel the true nature of my suspicious loitering in front of the Iraqi embassy, a man emerged from the dark doors and ushered us all inside.

The small door opened up into a large white marble lobby. Another official in a dark suit and dark glasses sat in front of a bank of screens that showed CCTV footage of the front of the building from at least seven different angles. "How can I help you?" he asked.

The oldest of the group of would-be fighters, a man in his late 30s, spoke for us; "We want to fight against the Americans," he said.

"Well, you can't go directly from Egypt," the official replied.

I was surprised he didn't offer thanks and long-winded praise for their bravery, pan-Arab credentials and unshakeable Islamic faith as Iraq's foreign minister had done on television when asked about the support his country was receiving from ordinary Arabs.

"The government here has blocked all but official travel to Iraq. Instead, you need to go to Syria. You can get there without a visa. And when you arrive, find the Iraqi embassy. Someone there will help you," he told us matter-of-factly.

The official then asked why the group wanted to fight in Iraq. Our unofficial group spokesman took a step forward. His Palestinian scarf announced his political credentials even before he spoke. The reason, he told the Iraqi official, was that they wanted to do what Arab leaders had not been able to do; they wanted to protect Arab pride and honor. The group murmured in agreement. The official then looked behind the older man, at the younger members of the group. Another, younger, man said he wanted to humiliate the Americans on the battlefield so they would leave the region. A third said his aim was to protect the wealth of Iraq so it could be used for the benefit of the Arab world. When it came to my turn, I admitted that I was a journalist and said I wanted to document what was to come.

As we left the embassy, the group crowded round me in curiosity. Our shared experience had at least earned me a hearing. They wanted to know who I worked for and what I wanted to write about. Although Reuters is British – and therefore Western – it has an enviable reputation in the Arab world for impartiality and accuracy. Even more helpfully, it's seen as an important and influential organization.

Four of the group agreed to meet me later and tell me what had made them decide that Iraq's defense was worth risking their lives for.

Hisham looked as if he were the youngest in the group. He was about 18 years old. He told me he'd just started studying engineering at one of Cairo's state universities. I knew that even with top marks, as an ordinary young Egyptian job-seeker without the resources to bribe his way into a well-paid professional career, he would probably be driving a taxi if he stayed in Cairo. And that's if he was lucky.

Two years later, the Americans faced a brutal and vicious insurgency in Iraq. The blame, they said, lay not with the Iraqis they had come to liberate from Saddam but "foreign fighters" like Hisham and his friends. These highly capable and motivated men, the military said, streamed into Iraq from Syria.

Whenever I heard military officials later describe these men, I thought back to Hisham. With a pen sticking out of his top pocket and his thick glasses, he looked like a technician rather than a warrior. Hisham didn't even have a beard. Looking at him, I didn't think he'd be able to grow one if he tried. The other members of his group looked like what they were; a motley collection of idealistic students, taxi drivers and low-level office workers. They all believed that they had an Islamic duty to defend Iraq, but none appeared particularly Islamic. Hisham knew much more about celebrity gossip than he did about Islamic regulations. Hatim, the oldest in the group, was a great admirer of the greatest leader of Arab socialism, Gamal Abdel Nasser. Another man called Khaled, a secondary school Arabic literature teacher, composed love poems in his spare time and told me he hated the "fanatics who thought 'love' and 'romance' were dirty words."

Five years later, in the Gulf, a former Iraqi army officer told me what happened to most of the men like Khaled, Hatim and Hisham, "We'd thank them, hand them a broken rifle, and then put them on the frontlines where they wanted to be. Most died in the first bombing waves."

The reasons they gave for their decision to travel far from home and fight a superpower were based on a jumble of deeply held grievances. Personal ones – like the poverty of life in a corrupt dictatorship like Egypt – mixed with collective grievances like the role of the United States in keeping Muslim countries poor so that they could not challenge its power.

At the same time, their reasoning was often contradictory. Hisham wanted to fight to keep Western influence out of the Arab world, but it was clear that influence was a big part of the culture he eagerly consumed. Khaled wanted to restore Islamic law, but at the same time he condemned the most zealous supporters of that system as "ignorant thugs". Another member of the group spoke as if the Arab and Muslim worlds were the same thing. He didn't know that Indian and Indonesian Muslims far outnumbered Arabs, or that a large minority of Arabs weren't actually Muslim. The whole group thought Al Qaeda had nothing to do with the attacks of September 11, 2001. But at the same time, they admired Osama bin Laden for taking on the United States.

We sat in the café for several hours and talked about the state of the Arab world (which we referred to as if it by default included all other Muslim countries from Albania to Brunei). We talked about past glories and present failures, and settled on a familiar discussion revolving around who was to blame for the failure of the Arab (meaning Muslim) world to chart its own destiny instead of having the will of others imposed upon it.

I emphasized the failure of the countries' own societies, and the group heading to Iraq blamed the conniving of the West. Hatim, the wise man of the group, said something that I'd heard – in one form or another – many times before. "Whatever we do," he said to the table, "the West won't let us develop because they don't want us to take their power from them."

I'd heard that sentiment throughout my entire life. I heard it every Eid when family and friends gathered to celebrate the main festival in the Islamic calendar. In fact, I heard it whenever a Muslim conversation turned to politics – which was often. Until I went to university to study Arabic, I believed it too.

The Muslim world – of which the Arab world is just a part – is a diverse place. But there are two groups of people who talk about it as one monolithic block. One comprises of sensationalist public figures in the Western world who like to reduce issues to their most basic form. And the other is made up of men and women looking for the quickest route to popularity in the Muslim world.

In reality, the Muslim world is made up of people from different cultures, religious understandings, income levels, histories and large numbers who aren't even Muslim. But there is something that unites the world's billion Muslims that doesn't exist in the Christian world; a sense of having fallen from grace. From its birth in seventh century Arabia until only two hundred years ago, the world of Islam felt content and secure in its destiny as the pinnacle of human achievement. However, that sense of security and global identity was shaken by the rise of the West and its domination of Muslim lands.

This sense of collective wounded pride runs so deeply amongst the various and disparate Muslim communities of the world that it is often relied upon as a rallying cry by rebel leaders, unpopular politicians and commentators looking for an audience. It works because deep down it strikes a chord. For two hundred years – since Napoleon invaded and occupied Egypt in 1798 and the British strengthened their control over Muslim India a little later – the Islamic world has looked for answers for its downfall in the actions of others.

This very emotional sense of loss began almost straight after people in the Muslim world realized their new relative weakness compared to the Western world. Even new members – converts from Western society – were not immune from the immense sense of loss and dislocation along with almost a pining for a more glorious past.

Marmaduke Pickhall, the son of an English churchman, became a Muslim after travelling in the Islamic world at the turn of the 20th century. He is well remembered for having overcome the opposition of the traditional Islamic establishment to produce the first authorized and scholarly translation of the Quran. Even though he was not born into a Muslim culture and environment mourning its recent setbacks, he quickly adopted the same sense of loss.

In a speech in Cairo in 1929 at the Young Men's Muslim Association in Cairo, Pickhall told his audience: "Muslims felt despair because they were defeated. It was only natural. But was there any reason for despair?" He went on to compare the situation at the time to an episode in the early years of Islam when the Prophet Mohammed signed an unfavorable peace agreement with his Arab opponents. The treaty gave the early Muslims a period of quiet they used to strengthen their community. "The truce of al-Hudeybiyah, though it seemed so ignominious for the early Muslims," Pickhall argued, "was in fact the greatest victory that Islam had until then achieved ... For centuries of war had set a rigid barrier between the Muslim world and Christendom, and now that barrier is down, no matter that the terms of settlement seem ignominious to the Muslims. That settlement may yet prove to be the greatest victory that Islam has yet achieved."

Pickhall was speaking just a few years after the dismemberment of the Ottoman Empire, which was seen by millions of Muslims at the time as the ultimate humiliation of Islam. At around the same time, a man in Lahore who became the national poet of Pakistan – a country he didn't live to see – penned poetic laments about the state of Muslims that still resonate with millions in the Persian and Urdu speaking worlds.

One of Mohammad Iqbal's most well-known poems is called Jawab-e-Shikwa (A Response to a Complaint), where he presents a downtrodden Muslim almost castigating his Lord for abandoning his long-suffering worshippers after their great sacrifices in his name.

We impressed on every heart the oneness of our mighty Lord,
Even under the threat of sword, bold and clever was our call.

Who conquered, tell us, the fearful Khyber pass?
Who vanquished imperial Rome, who made it fall?

Forget about the forests, we spared not the seas,
Into the dark, unfathomed ocean, we pushed our steeds.

We removed falsehood from the earth's face,
We broke the shackles of the human race.

We reclaimed your Kaaba with our kneeling brows,
We pressed the sacred Quran to our heart and soul.

Even then you grumble, we are false, untrue,

If you call us faithless, tell us what are you?

You reserve your favors for men of other shades,
While you hurl your bolts on the Muslim race.

Iqbal then imagines God answering:

"We reward the deserving folks with splendid mead,
We grant newer worlds to those who strive and seek.

Arms have been drained of strength, hearts have gone astray,
The Muslim race is a blot on the Prophet's face."

"All of you love to lead a soft, luxurious life,
Are you a Muslim indeed? Is this the Muslim style?

All of you desire to be invested with the crown,
You should first produce a heart worthy of renown."

The poem is not forgotten literary history. Students in Pakistan, India, Bangladesh and even Iran and Afghanistan will learn verses at school. In Pakistan, Iqbal's poems, steeped in the imagery of loss and renewal, are frequently broadcast on television and radio.

The idea that Muslims have become "soft" and "unworthy" wasn't born with the collapse of the Ottoman Empire. Muslim histories are full of writers complaining – even at the height of Islamic power – that the people of the prophet had long abandoned his example. But these protests – like the indignation of 14th century traveler Ibn Batutta when seeing the unchecked consumerism of Cairo's Grand Bazaar – have the ring of a pensioner complaining "things were better in the old days". However, the collapse of the last Muslim empire on the world stage turned these thoughts from grumblings to transnational shock. The end of the Ottoman order suggested that Islam's day had gone and to people whose whole world outlook was shaped by the public and private spheres of a civilization that saw itself as the pinnacle of divine guidance, this meant being stuck between the reality they could see and the truth they felt in their hearts.

That "greatest victory" for Islam that Pickhall was hoping for didn't come. From the end of the Ottoman Empire to the present day, the people of the Muslim world have generally become poorer, less well educated, more likely to live in societies mired in violence and less likely to have a say in the way they are governed compared to people in other parts of the world. All the while, they compare there present humiliating status to the glories of the past.

The sense of humiliation gave birth to a succession of leaders who claimed to redress it. And for the most part, Muslim populations have proven willing to forgive many shortcomings if their leaders at least pay lip service to notions of regaining power and influence on the world stage. In the end, the Muslim world ended up with rulers who did nothing to change the sense of humiliation while making the lives of their people progressively worse. The more Muslim nations became tied to Western politics and economics for their survival, the less leaders could indulge their populations' desire to be free of Western influence – the cause, as they saw it, of the loss of their position in the world and the reason for their present lowly status.

At the moment, if a leader is to defy the West in any way, he's certain to win popularity. In 2006, Hassan Nasrallah of Hizbullah had to only draw in his war with Israel to achieve immense popularity. After all, he had done more than any other Arab and Muslim leader of the last 60 years to check Israel's regional power.

In Egypt, suspicion of Shi'ites, the Muslim tradition that Hizbullah belongs to, is increasing, but that didn't stop Nasrallah becoming a hero in the Arab world's most populous country.

Ahmed Fouad Negm, a leftwing Egyptian writer, poet and human rights activist, wrote a column in an Egyptian newspaper describing how he had watched a friend buy 20 posters of Nasrallah. "People are praying for him as they walk in the street, because we were made to feel oppressed, weak and handicapped," Negm said in an interview. "I asked the man who sweeps the street under my building what he thought, and he said: 'Uncle Ahmed, he has awakened the dead man inside me! May God make him triumphant!' "

Hizbullah is an Islamist organization, which means that its ideology is based around the idea of recreating the glory of an Islamic past by the application of the rules of Islam in private and public life. In its present form – which includes a wide variety of opinion from the centrist political party ruling Turkey to Osama bin Laden's al Qaeda – it is the latest manifestation of the Muslim world's struggle to address and halt its decline in the face of Western power. Islamism was born from the failure of the traditional Muslim world to meet the challenges of the modern world. As such, Islamism shares its birth with Arab socialism, Turkish nationalism, Iranian nationalism, pan Arabism and all other ideologies that have sought to recapture lost glories of a bygone world. Since they have a shared origin, it's not a surprise these ideologies share certain characteristics. Islamists think the key to an Islamic renaissance is the re-fashioning of society to adhere to Islamic law. Modernists – and this includes various forms of socialists, nationalists as well as the Muslim world's few liberals – think that the answer lies in adopting practices from the West. Both approaches seek a return to a lost grandeur. Political revolutionaries – Islamist and modernist – evoke the past to garner popular support. Secular nationalist movements reach back into a pre-Islamic history to evoke the glories of an even older age. But this is a case of superficial re-branding. The intellectuals of Ba'athism, Arab socialism or numerous nationalisms seek to break with the expectations that come with an Islamic identity, or to narrow their audience to just the people within their own geographical area. But they still promise to deliver the glories of the past.

No matter what the labels, secular and Islamist approaches tend towards autocracy and are extremely hostile to criticism and dissent. Neither has chosen to embrace the concept of constructive criticism. Both have an affinity for strong one-man leadership. In fact, the secular political parties in Egypt, Lebanon and Jordan (whether left wing or liberal) are often one-family organizations with decision-making left to a select, elite group that regular members have no hope of influencing. There is little, in practical terms, to differentiate them from the Islamist parties like the Muslim Brotherhood, which has a secret leadership committee that decides on policy and leadership. In each case, political platforms take a back seat to organizational culture.

Islamist or modernist, everyone is looking for easy answers. For followers of the Muslim Brotherhood, everything needed to govern everyday life successfully, whether on a personal or public level, already exists in a traditional reading of Islamic law. Modernists, whether they are meant to be socialists, communists or liberals, sacrifice ideology for unity. But both are seeking easy answers and avoiding difficult questions by blaming external forces for their condition. Both evoke a past they think was destroyed by hostile outside powers.

Simply, Hisham and his friends are the product of the Muslim world's 200-year old decline from the unchallenged supremacy it assumed was its God-given right. The sight of Western warships passing through the Suez Canal in their country on their way to subjugate another Muslim nation made it painfully clear how powerless their leaders actually were. In light of the impotence of their representatives on the world stage, the men who sought out a route to fight in Iraq decided to seek absolution from their collective weakness by making a grand gesture. And the depths to which their civilization had sunk – as proved by the warships – meant the gesture had to be dramatic.

But the "clash of civilizations" is not a foregone conclusion, because even though Muslims are taking refuge in unforgiving literalist interpretations of their faith, historically, this has never had long-term popular appeal. By understanding the roots of the Muslim world's outlook, we stand the best chance of finding a real solution to a spiraling international conflict instead of relying on repressive measures that further fuel the vicious circle and threaten civil liberties that politicians say they are fighting to preserve.

Chapter 1

The Decline

The Bedouin warriors of early Islam conquered land from Spain to India and ruled it through the office of a caliph, the leader tasked by early Muslims with running the affairs of the community. Although Muslims recognized from the earliest days that their states were not perfect, they were seen to be the best available method for organizing public and private life. As long as the ruler ensured a measure of social justice, stability and security he – and at times, she, – would be given loyalty. Muslim states, with the caliph as their figurehead, were the manifestation of Islam as a religion and a worldview. And, as long as they kept winning wars and protecting the lives, honor and wealth of the citizenry, Islam's position in the eyes of its followers as God's final word to man was unassailable.

Splits amongst Muslims developed soon after the death of Islam's founder, the Prophet Mohammed. A serious civil war between some of the prophet's closest followers was followed by the Shi'ite-Sunni division that remains until today. Sunnis maintained that leadership of the community should be agreed amongst the new community of Muslims. Those that became the Shi'ites saw it as the right of the prophet's descendents through his nephew Ali.

For more than a thousand years, Muslims, like people in the Western world today, accepted with little question that their way of life was the pinnacle of human achievement. The most well-known Muslim Empire in Europe was the Turkish Ottoman state, which survived until the end of the First World War in 1918. The Safavids of Iran and the Mughals of India were the other large Muslim empires of the later medieval age. As American politicians and intellectuals talk about the universal yearning for freedom, Muslims believed their system would be adopted by the world once everyone else understood its superior qualities.

The decay of the Ottoman Empire became visible in the late 17th century. In 1699, Ottomans ceded most of Hungary to the Hapsburgs under the Treaty of Karlowitz; the first major surrender of European territory by the Ottomans. The next year, the Ottomans, who had besieged Vienna only 17 years before, acknowledged Russian conquest of the northern shores of the Black Sea. After that, the Ottomans were on the defensive, but it wouldn't have seemed like it to the subjects of the Ottoman Empire. Sultan Ahmed III was prodded into another war against the Russians in 1710 and the forces of the sultan won a major victory at the Battle of Prut. In the grand scheme of things this victory was the spluttering comeback of a waning power. But such spluttering allowed the rulers to continue believing that their world wasn't really changing.

Life, in fact, carried on much as normal in the palace of the sultan for nearly a hundred years before the rulers of the empire were forced to accept Europe, the area of the world their ancestors had written off contemptuously, was posing a serious problem. The majority of the subjects of the Persian shahs and the Ottoman sultans could be shielded from the repercussions of losing territory but they couldn't avoid exposure to the reality of the decline of Muslim economic power.

European goods and the penetration of European economic control came ahead of military conquest. And like in India, it arrived through a gateway opened by a confident Muslim ruler who thought he was throwing a bone to the Europeans in the name of trade. European economic control came about in the Ottoman and Persian empires through treaties called Capitulations. The first was signed between France and the Ottoman sultan in 1536. The agreement allowed French merchants to trade tax-free in Ottoman territory and pay lowered tariffs for their imports and exports. The concession with the greatest long-term effect was the agreement that French merchants would be subject to French law under the jurisdiction of the consul rather than Ottoman Islamic law. At the time, considering the Ottomans allowed the various faith communities of the empire to be governed by their own laws, this wouldn't have seemed like a radical new prerogative to grant foreign nationals. However, as European power grew and Muslim power declined, the Capitulations were used by various European powers to wield huge economic and political power over the sultans and shahs in their own territories.

By the late 18th century, the changing relationship between the Europe and the Muslim world could be illustrated by a cup of coffee. Sugar and coffee were introduced to Europe by the Muslim world. Until the late 17th century, coffee was a major export from Muslim lands to Europe. By the early 18th century, the Dutch were growing coffee in their East Asian colonies (Java) and the French were exporting coffee from West Indian colonies to Turkey. Sugar, originally from India and Iran, was sold by merchants in Syria and Egypt to Europe. The Europeans took to growing sugar cane in their colonies more cheaply than it could be produced in the Muslim world and selling it back to Muslim traders. Historian Bernard Lewis mentions that by the end of the 18th century, around the time Napoleon landed in Alexandria, when an Arab or Turk drank his or her habitual morning coffee, the coffee and the sugar was grown in the West Indies or Central America and imported by French or English merchants. Only the water was locally produced.

Coffee and sugar are only two examples. Muslin from Damascus, cotton from Egypt and silk from India were no longer traded within the systems of the Islamic world. The raw material was grown in European colonies, the finance was arranged in the coffee houses of London and the ships carrying the goods were registered in Europe.

In Muslim lands, the new economic reality meant falling state revenues and rising inflation. State employees who were on fixed salaries suffered, and corruption seeped into the workings of the state. High and low posts in the empire became secured through the payment of bribes. The ambitious officials who rose to prominence would then try to recoup their costs by squeezing the ordinary people who had everyday dealings with the state.

As Muslim empires became poorer, their governance suffered and they entered a downward spiral. With less money in its coffers, the Ottoman Empire couldn't maintain its standing professional army, the Jannisaries, in the manner to which they had grown accustomed. The Janissaries were the professional foot soldiers of the Ottoman Empire. They were recruited at a young age from the non-Muslim peoples on the empire's borders with Europe. Young boys from Romania, Serbia, Bosnia, Hungary and elsewhere in south-east Europe were converted to Islam and trained and educated in religion, military know-how, languages and the arts. Those who were thought capable became Janissary soldiers – the first professional paid soldiery in Europe since Roman times. They were loyal only to the emperor and after their period of service were freed and given a pension but their children were not allowed to become Janissaries after them. Without any blood ties of their own, they were above palace intrigues and local politics in the regions they were posted to. But with the decline of the empire's fortunes, they came to stand for all the vices they were first established as an institution to avoid.

By the closing years of the 18th century, it had become more difficult to ignore the decline of the Ottoman Empire. They had already lost most of Hungary to the Hapsburgs in 1699. The following year, they lost the northern shores of the Black Sea to Peter the Great of Russia. Whatever sense of relief came from the occasional Ottoman successes in later wars with Russia and Austria was blown away by the Ottoman-Russian war in 1768. The Russian Baltic fleet destroyed the Ottoman fleet off the coast of Anatolia. On land, Russian forces drove the Ottomans out of Romania and the Crimea, which had been ruled by descendents of Genghis Khan as vassals of the Ottoman sultan. The Treaty of Kuckuk Kaynarja that followed in 1774 has been called by historians the most humiliating the Ottomans ever signed. As well as territory, the Ottomans had to contend with the trend of European powers chipping away at the internal power of the Ottoman state by seeking to become the protectors of non-Muslim subjects within the empire. Treaties that were founded by the Ottomans upon concepts of tolerance came to be used by outside powers as political instruments to further the often-competing aims of Europeans powers. Later Ottoman sultans became spectators of a game played on their soil that threatened to tear their country apart.

Napoleon's occupation of Egypt took place at a turning point in Europe's relationship with its religion and at a time Muslim society was trying to ignore its diminishing place in the world. Napoleon posed a threat that Muslims had not explicitly encountered before. This was not the in-your-face anti-Muslim Christian expansionism of the Crusades or the threat of annihilation posed by the unlettered Mongols. This was not even the Europe of Christendom. Napoleon represented a new player on the field – the West. Based geographically around Europe – with some newly acquired territory on a new continent – the West was a new set of ideas which announced it could live happily with Islam but still believed in its own superiority with the same zeal the old Europeans had upheld Christianity.

Instead of proclaiming the superiority of Christianity, as a Muslim population would have expected an invading French army to do, Napoleon went out of his way to sound Muslim. The first lines of his initial proclamation, which was printed in Arabic read: "In the name of God, the Merciful, the Compassionate. There is no God but God. He has no son, nor has He an associate in his Dominion." The first sentence was the Islamic formula stated at the start of Quranic chapters and customarily used by Muslims on a habitual basis. The second was nearly the Islamic declaration of faith ('There is no God but God and Mohammed is his messenger'), but not quite.

Napoleon states the local rulers of Egypt have "lorded it over Egypt (and) treated the French community basely and contemptuously, and have persecuted its merchants with all manner of extortion and violence." He then goes on:

> O ye Egyptians, they may say to you that I have not made an expedition hither for any other object that that of abolishing your religion but this is pure falsehood and you must not give credit to it but tell the slanderers that I have not come to you except for the purpose of restoring your rights from the hands of the oppressors and that I more than the Mamlukes serve God – may he be praised and exalted – and revere His Prophet Mohammed and the glorious Quran.

Napoleon set the trend of Western powers invading the Muslim world in the name of rights and freedom while serving their own national interests. Napoleon told the Egyptians that he was acting out of the goodness of his heart and the convictions of his country's new revolutionary principles.

Then as now, the locals weren't buying the propaganda. Egyptian historian Abd al-Rahman al-Jabarti wrote in his history of the French occupation:

> "'I more than the Mamlukes serve God...' There is no doubt that this is a derangement of his mind, and an excess of foolishness."

Jabarti was among the first Muslim observers to notice, with a pang of despondency, that the Europeans now had the upper hand in this new clash between East and West:

> The soldiers and the Mamlukes gathered on the two banks, but they were irresolute, and were at odds with one another, being divided in opinion, envious of each other, frightened for the lives, their well being, and their comforts; immersed in their ignorance and self delusion; arrogant and haughty in their attire and presumptuousness ... heedless of the results of their action; contemptuous of their enemy, unbalanced in their reasoning and judgment.
>
> They were unlike the other group, that is the French, who were a complete contrast to everything mentioned above. They acted as if they were following the tradition of the community (of the Prophet Mohammed) in early Islam and saw themselves as fighters in a holy war. They never considered the number of the enemy too high, nor did they care who among them was killed. Indeed, they considered anyone who fled a traitor to his community, and an apostate to his faith and creed. They follow the orders of their commander and faithfully obey their leader. Their only shade is the hat on their head and their only mount their own two feet. Their food and drink is but a morsel and a sip, hanging under their arms.

Jabarti was describing the scene before the Battle of the Pyramids. By the end of the brief encounter, 6,000 Egyptian soldiers lay dead compared to 300 Frenchmen. The rest of the army dispersed and Napoleon occupied Cairo. An Ottoman army that arrived to recapture Egypt was also destroyed by Napoleon. When Napoleon did leave Egypt in 1801, it was because the British navy had sunk his fleet in the Mediterranean and cut his supply lines.

Egypt hadn't been returned to Muslim rule by the actions of its inhabitants or the power of the Ottoman emperor. Instead of forming an alliance that suited the strategic requirements of the empire, the Ottomans had only been able to reclaim Egypt because it was in British interests to help them. Muslim self-determination had come to an end.

In 1799, while Napoleon was still in Egypt, Tipu Sultan, the last Muslim ruler of an independent Indian province, was defeated and killed by the British at Seringapatam. The unfortunate Mughal Emperor of the time, Shah Alam II, spent 40 years trying to recapture the glory of the Mughal crown by adventuring around the states of northern and central India trying to raise armies and make alliances. The scion of the clan fathered by Timurlane launched half-hearted attacks on the forces of the East India Company and then begged for allowances. In 1803, British forces entered Delhi and made Shah Alam a pensioner of the British crown.

As the Ottoman Empire was floundering in Europe and the British had become the most powerful player in the subcontinent, the intellectuals of the Muslim world, many of who were also religious scholars, realized that the system of government and administration built up on Islamic rules and robed in an Islamic identity was on the way down. And its decline was a threat to Islam as a religion. How could Islam, the final revelation to mankind, find itself in an inferior position to the religions it had come to supersede?

Jabarti's brutally honest observation from the Battle of the Pyramids shows the first flash of a crisis of confidence. With the British in India and other European powers controlling other parts of the Muslim world, it wasn't long before the crisis was taking root in other Muslim societies.

Chapter 2

Denial

Emerging from colonialism, the many peoples of the Muslim world were united in their desire to forge countries that would regain the international standing they lost with the ascent of European power. The leadership they got was not up to the task. Some like the Egyptian leader Gamal Abdel Nasser, who became an Arab icon, tried unsuccessfully, but most were too absorbed in internal power struggles to fulfill the aspirations of their people.

The Muslim world's leadership has spent the decades since the demise of colonialism painting a picture of their relative political and economic position in the world that isn't exactly true. They have had to resort to manipulation to bridge the gap between the popular desire for progress and respect on the world stage and actual decline and increasing political impotence. Modern media became the tool of their deception.

For much of the last five decades, Muslim governments have been generally successful at presenting themselves as improving the lives of their citizens and succeeding in defending the honor of their nations on the world stage. For the most part, their populations have believed it because the public had little other access to information about the outside world. However, they also believed it because they wanted to. The people of the Muslim world wanted to know that they commanded respect on the world stage. Despite the traumas of losses to Israel in the 60s and 70s, inter-Muslim conflict and disastrous civil wars, Muslim populations were willing to believe their leaders were protecting their communal honor and advancing their interests on the world stage.

However, this became harder to maintain after 9/11, when

America upturned its low-key influence in the Muslim world to gather support for the invasion of Afghanistan and Iraq. For the small minority of people in the Muslim world who had the privilege of access to an international education, 9/11 prompted a new evaluation of the society around them. As income disparities had grown, the privileged minority had grown more distant from the lives of the masses. Believing the image projected by the regimes that progress was continuing unabated, those at the top of society were left with little understanding of their own countries.

In the summer of 2002, the United Nations Development Program (UNDP) provided the first comprehensive assessment of the Arab world's level of development and its standing compared to the other regions. Through cold, hard statistics, a group of Arab intellectuals led by Egyptian statistician Nader Ferghany charted the sorry tale of Arab intellectual and developmental decline. Although the report concentrated on the Arab world, it was understood that its findings represented the reality in every country with Muslim majority, regardless of its government's political outlook.

The core point of the report was that poverty is not just a matter of income. Nader Ferghany said in comments to the media at the time of the report's release that a lack of freedom, empowerment, and access to knowledge also made populations "poor". To reflect that approach, the report went beyond the four development measures used to measure poverty by the United Nations Human Development Index to include measures of social and political freedom. And by those measures, even in the oil-rich Gulf region, Arabs were amongst the "poorest" people in the world.

The report was provocative not only in the data it presented but also the manner in which it was presented. The Arab world's condition was directly, and unfavorably, compared to countries Arabs had assumed were less developed than them. The aim had been, the authors said, to shatter the complacency and denial ever-present in the Arab world's understanding of its own place in the global development league.

The report revealed that the Arab world's 280 million inhabitants lived in countries where economic output increased significantly only when oil prices were high. The oil price boom fuelled the rapid economic growth between 1975 and 1980. Between 1990 and 1998, economic growth mirrored a steadier rise in energy prices. Higher birth rates effectively cancelled out any increases in any case. Economic output per person rose by only 0.5 percent, which was effectively economic stagnation. The global average over the same period was 1.3 percent, which meant that living standards in the Arab world decreased relative to the rest of the world. The only region with poorer economic growth was sub-Saharan Africa.

But the biggest shock lay in the areas of education, science and knowledge, where, as inheritors of a great civilization Arabs assumed their countries would make at least a respectable showing. Illiteracy among adults in the Arab world is high by international standards, the report explained, and high even by the standards of developing countries. Moreover, the number of illiterate people in the Arab world was increasing. Private tuition and education had become paramount in enabling students to study subjects that would lead to a desirable career. The result, said the report, was that education was no longer a means to social advancement and instead had become a means to perpetuate social stratification and poverty. In terms of information and knowledge, the report noted that the Arab world translated only 330 books a year, just a fifth of the number translated by a small European country like Greece.

Limited literacy and access to information is coupled with a very low level of political participation. The report noted that in many countries in the comparable regions of Latin America, East and South East Asia along with sub-Saharan Africa, freedom of association was less restricted and government, from time to time, changed through the ballot box. The report said that when it came to freedoms in the form of civil liberties, independence of the press and political rights, the Arab world had the lowest score for all regions of the world.

Considering that freedom as a concept was always articulated in relation to the unbalanced and unfair relationship with European colonizers or America, it's not surprising that Arab governments didn't feel the pressure to grant freedoms at home. The result, as the report pointed out, was that the Arab world "is richer than it is developed".

The report made difficult reading, but Arab commentators could not wave away its findings in the same way they could have hidden behind patriotism and pride to avoid similar conclusions if they had been made before 9/11 by a foreign country or an institution seen as Western, including rights organizations such as Human Rights Watch or Amnesty.

The editor of the Saudi-run Arab News Khaled al-Maeena said the report should be made compulsory reading for all Arabs. Salaama A Salaama, of Egypt's state-run al-Ahram, said the report needed a "serious, deep reading" because "no changes will occur without Arabs first facing the facts, however unpalatable they might be."

The report did shock many professional Arabs across the region, who realized that they had effectively been ignoring large parts of their own countries. This wasn't only true for the governments, but also for the small segment of the ruling elites of the Muslim world who had access through their privileged economic status to educations, jobs and travel opportunities denied to the masses. But the internal, long overdue, debate that the report kicked off was cut short by the US-led invasion of Iraq and George W. Bush's use of the report to press for the neo-conservative plan to bring change to the Middle East. But the report served its purpose. Introspection was not the only new development needed in the Arab world. A change of perception of the relationship between the rulers and the ruled was also necessary.

President George W. Bush, much to the authors' dismay, leaned on the report to make his case for the sort of change he wanted to see in the Muslim world. Ironically, it was the war he started to achieve that change which led Muslims to realize and resent just how much independence they had lost to the West.

The steady television coverage of warships moving into the region to attack Iraq in 2003 – and the inability of any Muslim government to stem it despite the cries of their populations – was a turning point. The build-up for the invasion shook the relationship between the rulers and the ruled in Arab countries.

The Egyptian government doesn't usually allow demonstrations. But it felt that allowing people to express their anger would serve as a warning to America and allow an outlet for the pent-up frustration. At the same time, it hoped desperately that same frustration would not find a new target in the form of the government. The government had reason to be nervous. Before America started gearing up for war, most Egyptians were not fully aware of the nature of their country's relationship with America. Thirty people polled at random for an article I was writing thought their country was self-sufficient in food and took no aid from the European Union and the United States, when in actual fact, Egypt took about $2 billion in economic and military assistance from Washington and was one of the world's largest importers of wheat. At about the same time, al Jazeera was offering a running commentary on every American and British warship to pass through the Suez Canal. This particularly stoked anger amongst Egyptians, who thought their government had the power to refuse these vessels passage through the waterway. Every Egyptian school child is taught how Gamal Abdul Nasser restored national pride by retaking the canal from the British and bringing it under full Egyptian control. The images of the ships passing through the canal to attack a "brotherly Arab country" so incensed public opinion that Egypt's President, Hosni Mubarak, had to tell the public in a televised speech that the canal was an international waterway and he could not stop vessels passing through it. "It would be different if they were declaring war on me," he said very seriously.

In the weeks before the war, I was sent to Cairo's doctors' union, where an anti-war demonstration was taking place. When I reached the union building it was surrounded by at least 10 times as many riot police as there were demonstrators ringed inside. My bureau chief had said "don't just go ask a few questions and come back. Talk to people, get an idea of what they are thinking, get into an argument. Even if you don't come back with a story, it will help you understand what's happening and you don't know who you'll meet again." I didn't get a story and ended up causing an argument.

The small courtyard was packed with about 500 people. Two men, one a bearded religious figure and another a younger activist, stood on crates at opposite ends of the courtyard and competed for the crowd's attention. I asked a man near me what the demonstration was about, and he said, "We are against the war that America wants to fight against Iraq." I asked him what the people gathered at the demonstration were going to do about it. And he said, "We want to go and fight the Americans with our Iraqi brothers." By which time, a small crowd was gathering around us because everyone wanted the chance to vent their views to the international press. I asked what was stopping them from going to fight. And he replied, "Israel and America." The crowd murmured in agreement. So I pointed at the riot police outside and said; "Those aren't American and Israeli soldiers stopping you from leaving this building." Every one of the 500 people in the crowd was listening to the conversation between me and about five men in front of me. The two men standing on the crates had stopped shouting to listen in too. The crowd erupted and suddenly a multitude of voices were shouting and jabbing their fingers into my chest or patting me on the shoulders to get my attention. The strain of making his anger heard was too much for one man. I felt his grip tighten on my shoulder to the point of pain before I looked at him and realized he was having a seizure. Two men standing next to him carried him outside and the shouting resumed. I could only hear the odd words; "America", "protect", "Israel", "Saddam" and "hero" seemed to be the gist of it. Unable to make sense of all the voices, I kept shouting back "but who's stopping you from fighting for Iraq?" Finally, the voices died down slightly as I said many people around the world felt the war was wrong, but what I wanted to know was why they couldn't carry out their desire to defend Iraq. Finally, one teenager from the back said, "Well, it's our government isn't it. It does what the Americans tell it." Immediately, the crowd turned to look at the young man and someone hissed; "Shut up. He's a journalist from a British organization" and then turned to me and grinned.

Every now and again, a government with Western ties like Egypt or Saudi Arabia undertakes a showboating exercise to prove its independence to offset the pro-Western policies that ensure its survival. One such incident took place on an actual boat in Cairo in May 2001. The case known as the Queen Boat trials involved the raid of a popular gay nightclub in Cairo and the arrest and trial of 52 men. The men were charged with "habitual debauchery", "obscene behavior" and contempt of religion. Details of the case were leaked to the local press, who accused the men of being Israeli agents seeking to destabilize Egyptian society. The idea that the men were part of a wider foreign plot was taken very seriously in a society that had come to think of homosexuality as an exclusively Western phenomenon. The government managed to outflank the Islamist Muslim Brotherhood by claiming to defend higher Islamic credentials while facing only muted criticism from international gay rights groups. Domestically, the local rights organizations found themselves so effectively outmaneuvered that they were unable to vocally defend the men's human rights for fear of tarnishing all their other campaigns in the public eye.

State control of information (and the cynical manipulation of the system of justice to further the state's ends) resulted in a strange gap between what people wanted to believe and reality.

By 2005, the inability of Muslim governments to keep up with the new sense of grievance was clear. One brilliant example of a regime's floundering can be clearly seen in the writings of a certain Samir Rageb, who was editor in chief of Egyptian newspaper al-Gomhurriya, one of the main directly state-run titles. Rageb lost his job later in the year after decades of service to the regime. His last columns were written as the state faced the prospect of popular internal criticism from middle class liberal Egyptians. His articles against the activists of the Kefaya! (Enough!) movement show how outdated the government's spin methods had become in the new post-Iraq war domestic scene.

> Whenever we follow President Mubarak to places of bounty, growth and prosperity ... we are compelled to sincerely believe that lapping water flows only from springs gushing with purity ... purified by his heart, intellect and honesty.
>
> Those who carry the "Kefaya" slogan, I say to them, enough with your self-loathing. You are full of spite towards those who are more valuable, wiser and knowledgeable than you. To the owners of "Kefaya": enough stupidity, naivety and ignorance.

Rageb was replaced in an overhaul of the state-run media apparatus shortly after this column was printed. But he had spent decades editing his papers, the most widely read in the country. For most of that time, he had been able to fulfill the state's needs by writing gushing praise. But it was no longer enough.

Chapter 3

Lost Glories

Seeing their governments' lack of clout on the world stage so graphically displayed, the bygone ages of Muslim power became a refuge and an aspiration for growing numbers of people in the Muslim world.

Maajid Nawaz describes himself as a former radical Islamist. Now, he works against extremism through the Quilliam Foundation in London. I attended a debate in London where Nawaz explained how he turned to extremism believing that the glory of Islam had been snuffed out by Western powers.

"I believed that we had been denied our identity as Muslims and instead had this common bond replaced with tribal allegiances to Western colonial constructs such as Pakistan, Syria, Egypt or Saudi Arabia," he said.

> Before this tribal identity had been forced upon us, we were one global super power. An umma that could protect its own from the kinds of things happening in Bosnia or Israel. I felt that this power had been taken from us by deliberate Western action. And, if it was taken from me, I needed to reclaim it. I believed that in Britain, the establishment taught me to be British because it wanted me to identify with the colonialists and not my oppressed brothers.
>
> I thought, "let's looks at the Muslim world. It's a collection of tin pot dictatorships propped up by the former colonialists. Who placed these rulers in power? Of course, the British. They put these incompetent leaders in place purposefully to keep my people weak."
>
> I believed Islam gave me the ideology to address these

> problems. It came with a detailed command and control system, a judicial system. The scripture was a perfect system to assert my identity, to resist colonialization. This was the solution to my identity problem.
>
> I decided it was my duty to oppose these dictatorships and be willing to sacrifice my life like the prophet and his companions to establish the umma on the ashes of the Muslim countries.

When Muslims imagine their shared Islamic past, accurate accounts of undoubted power and luxury become intertwined with fantasy of the righteousness of the society of the medieval Islamic world.

The Tulip Era between 1718 and 1730 was known as the height of Ottoman opulence. Court life became a big celebration surrounding the tulip-growing season. This is how the French ambassador described an evening at the house of the Grand Vizir Damad Ibrahim Pasha in 1726.

> When the tulips are in flower and the Grand Vizir wished to show them to the sultan ... Beside every fourth flower is stood a candle, level with the bloom and along the alleys are hung cages filled with all kinds of bird. The trellises are all decorated with an enormous quantity if flowers of every sort, placed in bottles and lit by an infinite number of glass lamps of different colors .... The effect of all these varied colors, and of the lights which are reflected by countless mirrors, is said to be magnificent. The illuminations, and the noisy consort of Turkish musical instruments which accompanies them, continue nightly so long as the tulips remain in flower.

The ambassador went on:

> Sometimes, the court appears floating on the waters of the

> Bosphorus or the Golden Horn, in elegant caiques, covered with silken tents. Sometimes, it moves forward in a long cavalcade towards one or another of the pleasure palaces ... These processions are made especially attractive by the beauty of the horses and the luxury of their caparisons. They progress with gold or silver harnesses and plumed foreheads. Their coverings resplendent with precious stones.

But that idealized image of Muslim power and wealth also included practices and views that would be considered un-Islamic today. The Ottoman social system, as in other Islamic societies, was made up of Sufi orders. Some held beliefs that were hard to reconcile with traditional Islamic practice. The Bektashi order in Ottoman Turkey had a large following among the state's Janissary corps, many of whom openly drank wine and encouraged their wives not to wear veils. The Bektashi, the upholders and defenders of Islamic power, would be seen today as indulging in imported Western practices.

Muslims in Turkey and the immigrant communities in Europe are fascinated with the power and glory of the Ottomans. Such accounts of Ottoman life fill editions of newspapers in Turkey, Bosnia and Albania as well as those in Pakistan. A children's cartoon on the life of the Sultan Fatih, the Ottoman sultan who conquered Constantinople from the Byzantines was translated and sold in Islamic bookshops across Europe and the Islamic world for a decade from the late 1990s. Muslim parents in the Islamic and Western world felt the need to present their children with a glorious Islamic past full of achievement because they felt it would "give them something to be proud of as Muslims."

In Egypt, Syria and the Palestinian Territories, the Mamluke dynasties of Muslim slave soldiers who built an empire and defeated the Mongols are celebrated in soap operas and the popular history books that are found on street corners. The fascination with a former glorious past is understandable if you feel your faith, way of life and civilization is humiliated in the modern world.

In the 11th century, the head judge of Toledo in Islamic Spain laid out the world view of classical Islam. Said ibn Ahmad was part of "Dar al-Islam", or the abode of Islam. He lived in Spain but his book was distributed and read in the university of Qayrawan in Tunisia, al-Azhar in Cairo as well as schools and universities of Baghdad, Herat in Afghanistan and Delhi in India. These centers of learning made up the intellectual backbone of Dar al-Islam. The geographical areas might be ruled by different sultans and amirs, but like Britain, Australia and the United States, the different political entities shared a world view, cultural reference points and a common basis of law.

Ibn Ahmed divides humanity into two camps – those with science and learning, and those without. Like civilizations before and after them, Muslims were preoccupied with identifying barbarians. It was the Greeks who coined the word in the first place – "Barbaros" – which meant the people whose language sounds like "bar bar bar". The idea being that everything that wasn't Greek sounded silly. The Muslims who came later borrowed the word – which became "barbari" in Arabic – and drew up distinctions of their own.

Eight nations contributed to the advancement of knowledge, as far as Ibn Ahmed was concerned; the Indians, Persians, Chaldeans, Greeks, Romans (which was used to refer to eastern Christians in general), ancient Egyptians, Arabs (which meant Muslims in general) and Jews. Some civilizations didn't make the premier league, according to Ibn Ahmed, but they did have some attributes. He praised the Chinese for their "crafts" and the Turks for their courage and skill in war. Everyone else, however, was beyond hope. What remained were the barbarians of the north in Europe and the barbarians of the south in sub-Saharan African. As far as Ibn Ahmed and general public opinion was concerned, they didn't have anything worth learning, trading or conquering.

Muslim scholars produced some of the most extensive research on geography in the pre-modern period. They concentrated on the parts of the world they traded with or the lands they wanted to conquer. Western Europe was ignored. In the late 9th and early 10th centuries, when the early Islamic caliphate still exerted power and its inhabitants thought the Islamic conquest of the world was a foregone conclusion, nearly nothing was known about Western Europe. Two of the best-known geographers of their day, who were meticulous in documenting Islamic lands and those of the Byzantines, felt no need to go further than hearsay when dealing with barbarians of the north. "In the sixth climate are the Frankland and other peoples. There are women there whose custom it is to cut off their breasts and cauterize them while they are small to prevent them from growing big," is what Ibn al-Faqih had to say in his book *Mukhtasar Kitab al Buldan*.

Ibn Rushteh at least knows of the existence of the British Isles, but doesn't bother himself with anything more. "In the northern part of the ocean are twelve islands called the Islands of Baratiniya. After that one goes away from inhabited land, and no one knows how it is."

In later years, the Islamic empires learnt a little more about the distant reaches of the earth but Masudi, whom Middle East scholar Bernard Lewis calls the "greatest geographical writer of his time", wasn't impressed. His comments about Europe display the same sort of casual racial stereotyping that writers in Europe and North America sometimes lazily apply to the Muslim world today:

> As regards the people of the northern quadrant ... The power of the sun is weakened among them, because of its distance from them; cold and damp prevail in their regions, and snow and ice follow one another in endless succession. The warm humor is lacking among them; their bodies are large, their

> natures gross, their manners harsh, their understanding dull, and their tongues heavy. Their color is so excessively white that they look blue; their skin is fine and their flesh course. Their eyes too, are blue, matching their coloring; their hair is lank and reddish because of the damp mists. Their religious beliefs lack solidity, and this is because of the nature of the cold and the lack of warmth. The farther they are to the north, the more stupid, gross, and brutish they are. These qualities increase in them as they go further northward.

Even centuries later, Muslims still saw little reason to acknowledge the existence of Europeans at all. All were referred to by the collective Afranj or Franks. Henry Timberlake, who published a book on his travels in the 17th century around Egypt and the Levant said; "The Turkes knowe not what you mean by the worde Englishman."

When most things worth seeing, owning or experiencing were available within Dar al-Islam, its people didn't think it necessary to look much further afield. A well-quoted statistic used to illustrate the American public's insular outlook states that only 24 percent of the population of the United States has a passport. The inhabitants of Dar al-Islam were even less likely to care about the outside world.

The lingua franca of Dar al-Islam was Arabic. Persian was spoken as a language of education and religion while Turkish became widely used for military affairs. An educated non-Arab would likely speak at least those three languages, and those from smaller ethnic groups would often speak four. Saladin, the Muslim hero of the crusades was a Kurd and so spoke Kurdish with his family. Amongst his generals and soldiers he would have spoken Turkish, and Arabic when it came to matters of state and religion. And like any respectable nobleman of his day, he would read works of poetry and mysticism in Persian. The three main languages of the Islamic world facilitated academic exchange and commerce. Ideas that sprung up in Delhi were quickly debated in Isfahan and rebutted in Damascus and Cairo. Goods, along with ideas, passed from one end of the Muslim world to the other. The common legal codes and languages made for a huge internal market that could keep a large trading class comfortable without worrying too much about the barbaric northern and southern ends of the world.

The Muslims who ran a confident, wealthy and expanding empire generally didn't bother with languages from outside the Islamic world. Christians, Jews and other non-Muslims living under Muslim rule translated the Greek books on science and philosophy and the Indian books on mathematics. Muslim rulers commissioned the works and expanded great effort in finding the books in the first place but it wasn't seen as the place of a learned Muslim intellectual to spend his time learning Greek. Latin speakers were so rare that the only way to read the introduction letter of an Italian ambassador to Baghdad in the 10th century was to root out a European convert working in the palace's clothing store.

Learning a European language wasn't a desired skill for a Muslim; you learned it because you had to. Either to pass the time of day with your captors or to trade insults with competitive fishermen in the Mediterranean. Learning Western languages was seen as a job for the non-Muslims of the Islamic world and as such there was a social stigma attached to it.

When people from the Islamic world – even if they weren't actually Muslim – met with Europeans, there was no doubt in their minds who it was that came from a "civilized" and "advanced" society with the power to dictate terms to the other.

Lebanese-American scholar Nabil Matar points out that Europeans were received in the Americas as Gods while in the Mediterranean they were made to feel inferior to Muslim military power. North African Muslim sailors operating with the tacit approval of the Ottoman sultan raided the English coast and boarded English ships which led to thousands of people being captured or sold into slavery. Joseph Pitts wrote an account in 1704 of the 15 years he spent in Muslim lands after his capture by raiders from Algiers. He describes locals staring at him in the streets and mocking him for resembling a girl.

England's Elizabethan government noted with alarm the vast sums of money that were having to be paid to ransom captives and the large number of families left destitute by the loss of the household bread winner. The English called the North African sailors pirates. The Spanish used the same world to describe Englishmen like Francis Drake attacking their treasure ships returning from South America.

Chapter 4

A Contested Heritage

Many Muslims today look back wistfully to an age when their societies and governments could afford to be dismissive of the Western world. But underlying that emotional reaction is the desire to return to an age when Muslims organized their societies according to systems that were developed internally, and so served Muslim needs instead of the desires of outside powers. The Muslim world had its own systems of rule built on the principles of Islam, customs from previous Greek, Persian and Indian civilizations and the needs of the day.

Muslim rule in the medieval period wasn't based on a monolithic set of instructions thought to be ordained by God. One of the earliest public issues to be debated was the role of the caliph, whose power had been chipped away towards the 11th century by sultans - provincial rulers who paid lip service to the authority of the caliph but often acted in their own best interests.

Sunni scholars adapted to this reality, combining tradition and reality. Al-Mawardi, who lived in the 11th century, supported the overall role of the caliph but went on to describe how authority should be delegated. From tax collection and agricultural policy to the personal and moral qualities required of each official, Mawardi laid out his blueprint for an Islamic government in detail.

As the power of the caliph became nothing more than ceremonial, the scholars again turned their attention on how the affairs of the Muslims should be run and decided that they themselves should work with secular authority as advisors and counselors. The religious establishment that grew up to fulfill this role saw its role as advising and admonishing the rulers to observe and implement Islam.

The Islamic world's concept of government started developing at an early stage in the history of Islam and then adapted and evolved according to the situation at hand. Central to that idea was justice. Al-Ghazzali, a revered Islamic political theorist and philosopher who lived between the 11th and 12th centuries, says in his *Book of Counsel for Kings* that rulers must act justly, ensure that their officials do likewise and uphold order, stability and Islamic law. The scholars of Islamic law developed, through the centuries, an independent check on the executive power.

Other centers of power also developed, such as trade guilds and Sufi brotherhoods. The Sufis center their religious observation on the mystical aspect of Islam. Throughout Muslim history they commanded the loyalty of millions of Muslims, had their own sources of income and at times were an irritant to the ruler. To this day, in many parts of the Muslim world Sufi orders play a huge role in society.

The Sufi practice of mixing religious observation with a deep popular desire to express closeness to God through mysticism and saint-veneration was – and still is – massively popular throughout the Muslim world. Sufi gatherings in honor of a saint are known by a number of names across the Muslim world. Amongst the most common are muwlid, milad and urs. Whatever they are called, the celebrations serve a similar purpose. They provide an opportunity to trade, and often the opportunity to indulge in drugs and alcohol in an attempt to get closer to God. A Sufi urs in Pakistan is nearly indistinguishable from one in Morocco. In the past, followers of other religions held similar celebrations alongside their Muslim neighbors. Sometimes, Muslims shared their saints with other faiths.

It is still possible to see a glimpse of the popular culture of the medieval Islamic world. In October 2003, as the Middle East was inflamed by reports of American and British soldiers killing Iraqi civilians, I visited a church in the Nile Delta that held a Muwlid every year in remembrance of St. George. The Egyptians I worked with at the time – both Muslim and Christian – couldn't understand why I'd want to see "a backward tradition of simple, uneducated villagers." They were also keen that I realized that as "modern" people they looked down on what they saw as superstitious practice.

After a bus ride of several hours, I reached a village with a huge church and a few simple shacks. I saw a line of people standing at the side of the church, away from the bright lights of the market stalls and the chanting and wailing coming from the main hall. I joined in the line not knowing what everyone was waiting for. Finally, a huge priest opened a side door and without exchanging words we all filed through a small door down a flight of steps.

Standing in a church crypt lit by a flickering light bulb, a veiled Muslim woman muttered Islamic prayers as a Christian monk tried to exorcise the demon she believed possessed her daughter. Other bearded, black-robed exorcists shouted into the ears of two groaning and vomiting Muslim women in another corner of the room. Muslims and Christians gathered in the underground vault to beseech the saint to help them banish the demons they blamed for afflicting their relatives. "It is well known God's power flows from their fingers," said the Muslim mother wearing a black headscarf and shawl, who would not give her name, as she watched the monks perform the exorcism on her half-conscious daughter.

Popular tradition says Saint George hailed from the north of the country. Some local Muslims believe the Quran makes veiled references to him as a holy man. Scholars say Christian traditions surrounding the saint seeped into the Muslim faith when it spread in Egypt after 640 AD.

In the subcontinent, Muslims sometimes share shrines with Hindus, who – according to a strict interpretation of Islamic doctrine – are not "People of the Book" like Christians or Jews.

Some of this popular practice embraced customs that were far removed from orthodox Islamic teachings. The shrine of Madho Lal Husain near Lahore is one such example. It houses the graves of two male lovers, Madho, a Hindu, and Hussain, a Muslim, who were so close that they are today remembered by a single name. Some residents of Lahore – and by no means a small invisible minority – will happily tell visitors about the unconventional relationship between the two that angered the pundits and mullahs but won the hearts of the masses.

The guilds of the Muslim world played a more official role in the organization of Muslim societies. The Ottoman Empire stipulated that each artisan must belong to one. At the height of the empire, the guilds and the market judges controlled the prices of the land. Traders were not allowed to earn more than 10 percent profit and those who swapped brain meat for suet or sold goods underweight were severely punished. The guilds were an immense source of independent influence.

Charitable foundations, or Awkaf, were also run with little state interference. Historians say a huge amount of the Ottoman Empire's wealth disappeared into endowments that supplied a massive range of public services in perpetuity. The sick could get free treatment, travelers could receive three nights with food in a hostel and the mentally ill were sent to asylums. Charitably minded donors would build shops or other revenue generating enterprises and bequeath their income to a cause. In this way, shops in a small town might finance the local drinking fountain or the upkeep of a vital bridge. Others in larger towns in Ottoman Europe might pay for food for poor pilgrims in Mecca.

The brotherhoods, guilds and scholars acting as check on the executive formed the basis of the kind of institutions a well-governed modern state would need. But these institutions, which were organic to Islamic society, were uprooted and destroyed in the drive to catch up to the West. The prevailing idea among the sultans, shahs and kings who tried to hold back the tide of

Muslim decline was that Western states were more centralized and this was one of the secrets of their success. After independence from colonialism, the rulers decided these independent centers of power were an obstacle to the much-needed modernization they needed to undertake.

The Muslim world of today is ruled by kings and presidents who are fully convinced that total control is the only way to secure advancement. The old forms of governance have become departments of the governing administrations and staffed by officials who recognize that compliance is the way forward.

The structures of the past had no chance to develop into modern, stable forms of government that are rooted in the history and traditions of their populations. The checks and balances of modern rule were allowed to develop in the West into parliaments, a judiciary, a free press and non-governmental organizations. But in the Muslim world they were stifled. The irony is that Muslim nations are now being called upon to adopt these same measures from Western experience but many resist because they see them as Western un-Islamic imports.

Chapter 5

Fighting Back

The first real threat to the existence of the Islamic world was not European and Christian, but Asian and pagan.

In the 13th century, a great chunk of the Muslim world suffered death and destruction at the hands of the Mongol horde. Only Turkish slave soldiers ruling Egypt kept them out of the corner of the Islamic world west of Jerusalem. But between India and Syria, they wrought devastation on a massive scale.

Genghis Khan led the first phase of the Mongol thrust. In the 1220s, his horsemen attacked and razed the trading cities of Samarkand and Bukhara in Central Asia before moving onto Iran. In 1256, the Mongols launched a new campaign against the Muslim world under Hulagu, the grandson of Genghis. Two years into the campaign, Hulagu captured Baghdad and killed the caliph, the spiritual leader of the Muslim world. As the seat of the caliph, Baghdad was the cultural and political center of the Islamic world. Legend has it that the Islamic world's figurehead was rolled in a carpet and trampled to death by horses in his capital. After laying waste to the capital of the Islamic empire, the Mongols looked set to sweep across the remaining Islamic lands and make Muslim rule a memory. The Mongol horde was stopped from its aim of conquering Egypt by the last ditch effort of the Mamlukes at Ain Julut in present-day Israel in 1260.

Historians say the physical impact of the Mongols was devastating. Ira Lapidus calls it a holocaust. "The populations of many cities and towns were systematically exterminated," he says. "Whole regions were depopulated by invading armies and by the influx Turkish and Mongol nomads who drove the peasants from the land. The conquerors plundered their subjects, made them serfs, and taxed them ruinously."

Mongol rulers, when not making skull pyramids outside the cities they had sacked, opened communications with the kings of Europe and discussed joint attacks on Muslim territory. In the minds of the Muslims of the time, the Mongols threatened the very existence of Islam by threatening to kill its followers and destroy its civilization. The crusaders of previous generations were little more than an embarrassing irritant in the grand scheme of things. Their power was never likely to spread beyond the coastal regions of the Levant. The Mongols on the other hand had already sacked the capital of Islamic power and seemed to be pausing for breath before finishing off the rest.

Desperate times called for desperate measures and the Muslim world's reaction to the Mongol invasion was the ideology of Taqi ad-Din Ahmad ibn Taymiyyah. The scholar who came to epitomize austere Islamic practice for the next eight centuries was five when in 1268 a Mongol army attacked his hometown of Harran, near what is now the border between Turkey and Syria. Like many thousands of others – Muslim, Jewish and Christian – living in the path of Mongol territorial ambition, Ibn Taymiyyah's father moved his family to the territory of the Mamlukes, who had become seen as the defenders of Islam.

Ibn Taymiyyah decided that continuing with present practice would lead the Muslims to slaughter at the hands of the Mongols. To deal with the very real threat the Mongols presented, Muslims needed to get back to their simple, ascetic, warrior past and rid themselves of the trappings they had picked up from the civilizations they had conquered. The young sheikh declared himself a mujtahid, a scholar qualified to undertake ijtihad – the independent interpretation the establishment said was no longer possible. Central to his Islamic outlook was the role of jihad. The lesser jihad, or warfare to defend or spread the faith, had taken a back seat in the classical Islamic world where

Muslim power felt comfortable and secure of its position. Instead, of seeing jihad as a strict military obligation on the Muslim authorities to wage war on their non-Muslim neighbors until the entire world accepted the superiority of Islam, the religious establishment took the position that the command to fight had been superseded by the greater jihad – an inner, moral struggle. The Sufi mystics spreading Islam at the time from the islands of Sumatra to sub-Saharan Africa developed further the idea of jihad as an inner struggle to become closer to God.

Ibn Taymiyyah parceled up whatever actions he thought were needed to save the Islamic nation into his definition of jihad. Compromise was as much a corruption of public life as the bribery and nepotism seeping into administration. "It is a duty for anyone who directs any part of the public affairs of the Muslims, Ibn Taymiyyah said,

> ... to employ the most suitable person he can find in each position which is under his control... If he rejects the worthiest and most proper candidate in favor of another, because that other is his relation, friend or freedman, or because they belong to the same country, legal sect, religious order or ethnic group – Arab, Persian, Turkish, Anatolian – or because he has accepted a bribe or service from this man, or for other reasons ... he cheats God, and His Prophet and the faithful.

Ibn Taymiyyah's ideology was not in favor of justice for its own sake. His entire outlook was shaped by the threats to Islam that he saw around him. An improved public administration was the upside, but the downside involved a rigid and unforgiving outlook towards others. As in communism and fascism, the desires of the individual were subsumed by the requirements of whole. He justified wars against the non-Muslim sects of the Levant and was suspicious of Jews and Christians. To enhance unity in the far-flung reaches of Muslim governance he wanted Persian, Turkish, Kurdish and Indian Muslims to adopt Arabic in their everyday speech.

Ibn Taymiyyah identified non-Muslims as the enemies of Islam and categorized them into four groups. Christians and Jews had a degree of tolerance as "people of the book" – the religions recognized by the Quran as sincere if misguided. Muslims, according to Ibn Taymiyyah, could share meals with this group of infidels, make peace agreements with them and marry their women. If they were captured in battle, their lives could be spared. The harshest treatment was reserved for Muslims who Ibn Taymiyyah saw as outside the fold. This included Muslims who had adopted un-Islamic habits. Peace with them would mean accepting their habits, which was unacceptable, so they could only be fought until they changed their ways. Muslims who Ibn Taymiyyah thought had rejected Islam while still claiming to belong to it were the epitome of hypocrisy and deserved no mercy.

The heavy price in freedom of thought that Ibn Taymiyyah demanded in return for an Islamic revival was too high for most Muslims. Like the austere ideologues hoping for revival today, Ibn Taymiyyah was swimming against the tide. Muslims, even in the golden age of Islamic civilization, mixed pre-Islamic customs and bent the rules of Islamic sobriety. Sometimes, as with saint veneration, they excused un-Islamic practices as actual religious devotion.

Ibn Taymiyyah saved the sharpest of his criticism for Muslims who visited the graves and tombs of deceased scholars or mystics. It was common, and is still widely popular, for rich and poor Muslims to visit these graves and pray to the deceased to intercede with them before God. Saint veneration was worthy of excommunication in Ibn Taymiyyah's eyes. But in the traditional Islamic world, saints' birthdays and tombs formed the infrastructure of public events. Sufis, like Christianity in Europe, adopted the veneration of gods and holy men of older religions. Ibn Taymiyyah wanted them stamped out as a heresy, and an affront to the central monotheistic principle of Islam.

In the modern era, although his teachings have found new followers, Ibn Taymiyyah's dogmatic approach and intolerance is still too much for most Muslim societies. In his own time, he was often in trouble with the state authorities. In 1298, the religious authorities accused him of questioning established theology and attributing human characteristics to God. The same charge in 1306 earned him 18 months in Cairo citadel's prison. Two years later, he was jailed again. In 1326, he was jailed by the government in Cairo in the Damascus citadel for condemning the veneration of saints despite having been warned not to.

What made Ibn Taymiyyah unpopular was his approach rather than the basis of his sentiment. The urban intellectuals of the Muslim world, whether in Morocco or India, saw saint veneration as a superstitious deviation with little place in the true faith but recognized it as a comfort to the peasants in the fields. In some cases, performing pilgrimages to the tombs of saints was a pastime of educated men. The great traveler Ibn Battuta heard Ibn Taymiyyah preach in Damascus as he visited tombs along his tour of the Islamic world. The great and the good of the medieval Islamic world could theoretically agree that praying by tombs wasn't exactly Islamic but they didn't think the pilgrims deserved to be put to death. The present-day followers of Ibn Taymiyyah suffer a similar obstacle to widespread appeal. Al-Qaeda's pronouncements against the injustice of the West and the slavish capitulation of Muslim leaders resonates with the Muslim masses but Osama Bin Laden and Ayman al-Zawahri's antidote of puritanical religious observation and the curtailing of freedom of interpretation finds limited popular appeal as it runs counter to centuries of popular understanding and practice.

Chapter 6

Ideas Old and New

At the core of Ibn Taymiyyah's ideology is the need to militarize and fight back. All else services that central aim. In the days of Islam's first conquests, the impulse was to incorporate and adapt. To survive, Ibn Taymiyyah thought, Islam needed to retrench and expel.

When Europe returned to the Muslim world in the eighteenth and nineteenth centuries as a newly reconfigured force with new ideas and the power of modern science and organizational skills behind it, the need to reform to survive was again felt throughout the Muslim world. As Muslims saw European soldiers on their soil, the ideas of Ibn Taymiyyah, which had been forgotten for centuries, began to be circulated once more.

Napoleon's easy occupation left once-confident Muslim societies grasping for answers. They knew they needed to change if they were to resist the military, economic and ideological power of this new enemy.

The governments of the Ottoman, Persian and Mughal empires decided the answer lay in adopting more of the West's methods, while rebels within those lands took up the banner of resistance based on Ibn Taymiyyah's approach of retrenching behind austere Islamic practice. A pattern was set which continues to this day and divides the Muslim world roughly between those who seek to redress the power imbalance by copying the West and those that seek a return to "pure Islam".

In 1802, a year after Napoleon left Egypt, Bedouins acting under the guidance of Arabian preacher Mohammad Abd al-Wahhab, crossed into what is now Iraq and attacked Karbala, the most sacred Shi'ite shrine, containing the tomb of the prophet's grandson. A year later, they sacked Mecca itself and after that Medina. In 1804, they attacked Mecca again and occupied it. The attack was a huge embarrassment to the Ottomans, who were the protectors of the holy sites and overlords of Arabia. The Wahhabis of the Saudi clan, who followed on from Ibn Taymiyyah's teachings, challenged their religious, as well as military authority. Over the next decade the Ottomans sent military expeditions out to deal with the threat with varying success until an Egyptian army completed the job for the sultan in 1818.

The Ottoman Empire's Tanzimat reforms, which happened at about the same time the Wahhabis were sacking and killing across Arabia, were a concerted effort to regain Islamic dignity by borrowing from the modern world. By the 19th century, the Ottomans saw Europe as the center of all things progressive and advanced while being painfully aware that the once great empire was seen as backwards and corrupt. The Ottoman Tanzimat reformers wanted to centralize the empire in its administration, culture and identity. This involved abandoning the Ottoman understanding of a multicultural and multifaith society where the different groups were united in their obedience to the ruling household, in favor of a Western concept of citizenship.

The reforms produced sectarian conflict. In 1860, fighting broke out between the Maronite Christians and Druze around Mount Lebanon. In the same year, Muslims massacred Christians in Damascus. The violence gave the Ottomans a chance to project themselves, civilized modern men of Istanbul, as the upholders of the law of a modern state that was working to civilize some of its more "underdeveloped" inhabitants. In the presence of European representatives the Ottoman Foreign Minister Fuad Pasha dealt with the aftermath of the violence in a way he felt was in line with European ideals of effective government. Surrounded by soldiers of the state in Western-style uniforms, he held what were supposed to be impartial tribunals that hastily handed down death penalties on scores of Muslims in Damascus. Pointing to his actions, Fuad Pasha claimed the Ottoman state was tolerant, and had always been tolerant, so could therefore claim to be a modern and civilized power as much as any European state.

The irony is that the Ottomans were trying to fight off the image the Europeans had of them as barbarous, emotionally stunted and irrational by shifting that image onto the people who inhabited the further ends of the empire. The reforming Ottomans of the 19th century developed their own "Ottoman burden". They began to promote themselves to Europe as "civilized" by shifting the Western image of "barbaric Asiatics" on the unequal people who lived far from the civilizing influence of Europe.

One female Ottoman teacher who was sent to work in Arab provinces during the dying days of the empire echoed the same patronizing racism as the British officials who were administering Egypt at exactly the same time. The difference between Turks and Arabs, thought Halide Edib, was that the Turk was a "natural leader" whereas the Arab was "naturally corrupt". The Turk was more European in manner rather than Eastern because Turks have been historically and physically closer to Europe, she said in her diaries. In Jerusalem, she thought "there was a hot and unwholesome atmosphere, mixed with religious passion verging on hysteria. The Turk alone had a calm, impartial, and quiet look. He . . . stood calmly watching, stopping bloody quarrels and preventing bloody riots in the holy places."

Edib's outlook echoes among the elites who run Muslim countries today. In Cairo or Karachi, Western educated and English speaking Egyptians and Pakistanis will talk of the "uneducated" masses who need to be purged of their emotional and irrational tendencies before their countries are ready for serious democracy. The understanding is still very clearly stated that interaction with the West makes an individual balanced and reasonable enough to be entrusted with the responsibility of having a say in the way they are governed.

The Tanzimat laws set the mould for Muslim reform that tries to borrow from Western practices while presenting it as just another expression of "true Islam". The 1869 law that decreed the new relationship between subject and state without an overt reference to religion couched the new revolutionary idea as a move back to true Islamic practice; a sleight of hand that nearly every Muslim state now performs when it wants to pass a law that flies in the face of tradition. The reforms also established a view of the citizenry as a submissive constituency that listens and obeys rather than participates in governance. All political groups in the Muslim world have followed this understanding, whether they call themselves religious, secular, nationalist or communist.

Between the nervous piecemeal adoption of Western methods by the rulers of the Muslim empires and the violent rejection of Abd al-Wahhab's Bedouin warriors, new thinkers were emerging who expressed the popularly felt need for revival and tried to find a way of achieving it.

The first person to express the need for a revival of Islamic politics in international terms was Jamal al Din al Afghani. Steam and rail travel made it possible for him to see the key centers of the Islamic world at the very time they were falling under Western domination. He saw the failed Indian Mutiny, or rebellion, of 1857. In Iran, he agitated against the concessions his host was granting to European trading interests. He lived through the Ottoman Empire going through the Tanzimat reforms and witnessed the Ottoman defeat in 1877 at the hands of the Russians. In Egypt, he railed against the mismanagement of the country that led to the British takeover in 1882. All of the Muslim powers he saw were racked with financial mismanagement and administered by weak governments while beset by predatory foreign powers.

Afghani could be described as the first activist and thinker of modern political Islam. He saw, in Islam, the political means to counter the challenge the modern world posed to the independence and dignity of the Muslim world. But he wasn't wedded to doctrine. The method of his approach was the blending of Islamic political consciousness with Western rationalism in the hope of reaching the elusive magic formula that would reverse more than 100 years of Muslim decline. But he was not concerned with developing an Islamic political dogma or even adhering to traditional Islamic injunctions. Iranian-born scholar Roy Mottahedeh says lifelong bachelor Afghani "picked up female companionship when he wanted it without any show of religious scruples." His main theme was that European powers were able to dominate in Muslim lands by dissolving Islam's place in society. But he didn't spell out what he thought Islam's place in Muslim society should be.

In an article entitled "The Materialists in India", published in 1884, Afghani explained how he thought the British had wrested India away from the Muslims and why they tried to attack Islam to keep hold over their new dominion.

> When [the English] entrenched themselves in India, and effaced the traces of Moghul rule, they gave the land a second look, and found within it fifty million Muslims, each of whom was wounded in heart by the extinction of their great kingdom. They were connected with many millions of Muslims in the East and West, North and South. [The English] perceived that as long as the Muslims persisted in their religion, and as long as the Quran was read among them, it would be impossible for them to be sincere in their submission to foreign rule, especially if that foreigner had wrested the realm from them through treachery and cunning, under the veil of affection and friendship. So they set out to try to weaken belief in the Islamic faith in every way.

The idea that Western powers need to attack Islam to maintain their control over Muslim land and Muslim populations is still popular, which means that the call to "re-establish" Islam remains a rallying cry while its meaning is still vague.

Like the secular and religious reformers who came after him, Afghani thought the ignorance and poverty of the Muslim masses made the job of the Western imperialists easier. The answer he believed lay in modernized Muslim societies. He wanted roads and railways along with modern institutions and education systems. But he understood Muslim society could not just adopt these new developments. It had to understand the ideas that fuelled the new Western science and rationalism.

The rulers saw in Afghani a populist whose calls for Islamic unity had popular appeal and could be adopted for their own ends. But Afghani's serious dislike for unchecked rule and his view that these same rulers had through their corruption, greed and mismanagement contributed to the Muslim world's problems meant that Afghani was constantly falling out of favor.

Afghani's ultimate aim was to have the leaders of the Muslim powers he courted working together against Western control instead of falling one by one as they remained consumed with self-interest and rivalry. But the most enduring element of his program is the idea that the West is attacking Islam to ensure its own power and that Muslims need to get back to the "real Islam". Many millions of Muslims today agree with that sentiment, but they disagree over what "real Islam" actually looks like.

Modern-day Islamism and secular nationalism in the Muslim world lead back to Afghani.

During his time in Egypt, politically minded young men came to hear Afghani talk about theology, jurisprudence, mysticism and philosophy combined with warnings about over-powerful Muslim leaders, and the need to check European expansion through national and broader Islamic unity. One of these men was Saad Zaghlul, who later became the founder of the liberal

Wafd party, and Mohammed Abduh, a scholar with a traditional background, whose student's went on to found the Muslim Brotherhood, the world's largest and oldest Islamist organization.

After Abduh's death in 1905, the two strands of Muslim revivalist thought diverged. One path led to efforts to retrench and cut out everything seen as foreign imports to Islamic practice. The other path looked outside Islamic tradition – specifically towards the West - for new avenues towards reform and renewal.

In 1928, Hassan al-Banna established the Muslim Brotherhood. The organization has members in every Arab country as well as substantial representation in Western countries, including Britain. If free and fair elections were held across the Arab world, the Brotherhood, as it's called, would probably control the governments of Egypt, Jordan, Kuwait and possibly Syria while holding considerable power in other Gulf countries. Hamas, an offshoot of the Brotherhood organization, presently runs Gaza after winning the Palestinian parliamentary elections in 2005.

Banna came to Cairo from his home the rural Nile Delta in the 1920s. The city he saw was much more Europeanized than in Afghani and Abduh's time. Banna first saw Cairo at the height of Egypt's "Belle Epoque" which ended when Gamal Abdul Nasser's Free Officers abolished the monarchy in 1952.

In Banna's Cairo, Europeans formed a privileged class that had access to luxurious clubs, restaurants, hotels and homes that Egyptians would mostly enter as domestic help. Rich Egyptians, admitted into this world at a lower standing, would be competing to prove their "progressive" Europeanized tastes and manners. Cairene high society would seem to an ordinary Egyptian to be shedding its indigenous character and brushing the vast majority of the population under the carpet in an effort to ingratiate itself to Europeans. The traditional educations of men like Banna would not allow them to rise in a changing society and the skills of their communities would be increasingly crowded out of the economy by the industrially produced goods from the West. At the same time, they would see around them a widening chasm between rich and poor, with those like them, the vast majority of Egyptians, on the losing side. In such an atmosphere, an average Egyptian would find little he or she could gain from the Western influence on their country, and much they would have already lost.

The British military, economic and political presence fuelled resentment. One particular incident caused such a deep scar that al Qaeda's Ayman Zawahiri could rely on it stirring passions a hundred years later. Despite its deep resonance for Egyptians, hardly anyone in Britain recognizes the name Denshawai.

On June 13, 1906, five British Army officers out hunting pigeons near the Nile Delta town of Dinshawai angered villagers by killing birds they had domesticated, and according to some reports, starting a fire on the straw roof of a grain store with errant shot. When the enraged villagers tried to seize the officers' guns, they shot at them. The riot that followed left several villagers and two of the officers wounded. In the end, the officers were made to hand over their weapons as well as their money and watches. Two officers escaped, one of whom died of heatstroke away from the village. The village elders secured the release of the other officers. The British returned the next day in force, set up a tribunal and convicted 52 of the villagers of attempted murder. Four were hanged. Others were sentenced to prison with hard labor and flogged.

The Egyptian policeman who had been with the hunting party contradicted the soldiers' story that they had been invited to the village and had done nothing wrong. He told the court that the officers had fired at the villagers. Reports of what had happened in the village reached Britain and caused public outcry, but in Egypt the incident drew the urban middle class, the farmers, peasants and students together against the British presence and fired up the newly forming nationalist movement.

Banna's political outlook developed in this atmosphere of deep resentment against the occupying power, and the locals who served it. His answer was more Islam. He thought the survival of Islam as a religion and civilization depended on winning over the young. What was holding Islam back in the face of European onslaught, Banna concluded, weren't the traditional scholars but adoption of Western secular ideas.

In 10 years, the Brotherhood had half a million members in Egypt and a growing presence abroad. Banna build a complex mass movement with a strong institutional structure. Committees oversaw legal and financial matters. The Brotherhood had a wing that provided an increasingly impoverished population with social services while other sections spread the group's message among peasants, doctors and engineers. The genius of the structure was to build the apparatus that reached out to the population on top of already existing networks centered around mosques, professional guilds and social groups. Businesses set up through the organization helped fund its activities and establish schools and clinics that serviced the local communities from which they came.

An Egyptian government agent killed Banna in February 1949.

Chapter 7

The Rise and Fall of Muslim Liberals

Egypt and India set the tone for the development of revivalist thought. With large Muslim populations and a long history of urban intellectualism, the ideologies that governed the hearts and minds of the Muslim world started life amongst Muslim Indians or Egyptians.

Banna's organization survived him. Political Islam, or Islamism, had been born. But it wasn't a mass movement straight away. The Brotherhood grew steadily and the organization continued to provide social services to some of Egypt's poorest people. After the collapse of the Ottoman world order, it was the urban intellectuals of the Wafd party, under Saad Zaghloul, that molded the aspirations of the Egyptian masses rather than the religious men from the Nile Delta villages.

The party formed one of the three parts of power in Egypt, the other two being the king and the British. In 1919, the deportation of Zaghloul to Malta by the British authorities caused riots and strikes throughout Egypt that left 800 people dead. At the height of its popularity, in the 1920s, the Wafd could bring thousands of Egyptians from all walks of life onto the streets for the cause of Egyptian independence from the British.

After the First World War, the British tried to damp demands for independence by renegotiating Egypt's status from protectorate to ally. Egypt was declared independent from Britain in 1922, but London maintained control of Egypt's defense along with the policing and maintenance of the Suez Canal. To Egyptians the foreign domination of their political and economic life would have seemed no different.

But by the end of the Second World War, the wealthy,

establishment politicians of the Wafd party came to be seen as part of the problem. Their approach seemed incapable of securing real independence.

If the liberal nationalism of the Wafd seemed too much like playing the game by British rules, the masses looked to a new set of rules that could achieve independence and self determination. The two options still involved embracing or shunning Western influences, but the playing field was becoming radicalized. Those looking to adopt Western ideas to fulfill their aims were moving towards dictatorial left-wing ideologies, and those wanting to find the solution within Islam were espousing a rapidly politicized understanding of the religion that sought to return to an idealized Islamic past and brush away all outside influences.

While Britain and France were carving up the old Ottoman world, the Muslim world was watching nervously as Jewish immigration was increasing in Palestine. Public sympathy was on the side of the Arabs, a largely Muslim population but also including Christian minorities. European Jewish immigrants bought land and cemented their presence in area, which caused large-scale dispossession amongst Arab farmers. Arabs and Muslims throughout the region saw the influx of European immigrants and the rapid transformation of the area into what resembled a European colony as a taste of colonialism's true plan for the whole Muslim world.

As the conflict progressed, it began to crystallize the development of a specifically Arab identity, which had been more fluid and vague under the Ottomans. Palestine became a rallying cry because others in the region feared European rule would mean dispossession and exile for them too. In Arab countries, the popular answer to the plight of the Palestinians became Arab Nationalism, the idea that the territories that had been drawn up by the British and French should unite to form one Arab superstate. The young men who developed the ideology behind Arab nationalism wanted it to appeal to as many people in the newly defined Arab states as possible, regardless of whether they were Christian, Muslim, or any one of the smaller religious communities in Lebanon, Syria and Iraq, so they avoided referring to Islam. In resting on an ethnic identity, rather than a religious one, pan-Arab ideology looked towards socialism as its guiding principle. The ideology started taking shape amongst the Western-educated urban elites of Iraq and Syria before it was adopted by military men in Egypt. Arab countries looking to support the Palestinians founded the Arab League in 1944, but they couldn't prevent the expulsion of Palestinians from the country that became Israel in 1948.

In the early 1940s, Salah al Din al Bitar and Michel Aflaq developed another secular resistance and reform ideology based on Arab unity which became the Ba'ath Party. Ultimately, the only two Ba'athists to come to power in the Arab world, Hafez al Asad in Syria and Saddam Hussein in Iraq, used the ideology as a cover for their own ambitions.

In Egypt, the military men who blamed the king and the parliamentary government for their defeat against Israel staged a coup orchestrated by Gamal Abdel Nasser in 1952. One of their main complaints about the previous British-controlled liberal government was that it had tarnished Egypt's reputation in the eyes of the world. General Mohammed Neguib, the first president of the new regime, laid out the reasons for the revolution very clearly when he forced the king into exile. "In view of what the country has suffered in the recent past ..." he told Egyptians through a radio broadcast;

> ... The complete vacuity prevailing in all corners as a result of your bad behavior, your toying with the constitution, and your disdain for the wants of the people, no one rests assured of life, livelihood, and honor. Egypt's reputation among the peoples of the world has been debased as a result of your

> excesses in these areas to the extent that traitors and bribe-takers find protection beneath your shadow in addition to security, excessive wealth, and many extravagances at the expense of the hungry and impoverished people. You manifested this during and after the Palestine War in the corrupt arms scandals and your open interference in the courts to try to falsify the facts of the case, thus shaking faith in justice.

Nasser replaced Neguib shortly afterwards as president. The new president's ideas went beyond a simple change in government. He wanted to restore the honor of Egypt and the Arabs. Nasser called his new ideology Arab Socialism. And Egyptians were seduced by it in the millions. But Nasser wasn't a committed student of socialist ideology. He had flirted with the Muslim Brotherhood as a young man but it seems the Arab-Israeli war had pushed Arab nationalism to the forefront as the rallying call for a new, rejuvenated civilization that would finally restore honor and dignity. And socialism provided the ideological framework for a state-led drive towards industrialization and the elusive goal of modernization, which was needed ultimately to catch up to the Western world. It also helped that socialism was linked to the Soviet Union and seen as opposing the ideals of the West.

Nasser went from a popular Egyptian president to an Arab icon when he brought the Suez Canal under Egyptian control in 1956. Before then, Britain maintained troops to guard the canal, provided its management and kept most of the revenue from the international waterway. British control was a painful reminder that the old colonial power maintained control over one of Egypt's most valuable national assets and justified its presence by the pretext that Egyptians were not capable of operating and running the canal themselves.

Arab historian Rashid Khalidi says the Suez crisis established

Nasser as the pre-eminent Arab leader and his Arab socialism as the pre-eminent Arab post-colonial ideology. On July 26, 1956, during a speech in Alexandria, Nasser mentioned the name of Ferdinand de Lesseps, the engineer who designed the canal. The name was a prearranged signal to Egyptian forces to seize the canal. In the rest of the speech Nasser said the nationalization law had been published, the canal company's assets had been frozen and the British and French stockholders would be paid in full for their shares.

The move itself was dramatic and symbolic enough to fire nationalistic passions amongst the population. But the response from Britain and France really catapulted Nasser's popularity in Egypt, amongst Arabs and millions of others still living under or just emerging from colonial rule. Israel invaded Sinai in October 1956 under a secret agreement with Britain and France that the two European powers would then land forces in the area, separate the armies of the two hostile neighbors and then use the hostilities to argue the area around the canal needed to be administered by them. In the end, the United States used its diplomatic and political power to force an end to hostilities and leave the canal in Egyptian hands.

The perception in Egypt, the Arab world, the Muslim world and much of the rest of the developing world was that Nasser had stood up to Britain. In actual fact, the British and French had captured the canal zone with little difficulty but the Americans had threatened Britain with economic collapse. The Suez Crisis, as the incident came to be called, is referred to as the conflict that spelled the end of the British Empire. At the time, Nasser's millions of supporters wanted to believe the brave Arab leader had humbled the old superpower.

In 1967, Israel beat the armies of Egypt, Jordan and Syria during six days of fighting. The defeat cost the Arabs the remaining land they had held after the 1948 war, including Jerusalem and its al-Aqsa mosque, the third holiest in Islam. The defeat was a psychological disaster that sent the Arab, and wider Muslim world into shock and mourning. The combined Arab armies, which had twice as many troops, tanks and warplanes as Israel, had been beaten once more on the field of battle by a small fledgling nation. For the Arab states, the defeat was even more calamitous than the earlier war because the regimes that evolved out of the colonial period had staked their legitimacy on regaining Palestine for the Arab world. Egypt's Free Officers had justified their coup on the grounds that the previous government's incompetence had lost Palestine in the first place.

The Six Day war laid bare the reality of the "Arab revival" that had inspired the masses from Morocco to Iraq and worried the former colonial powers in Western Europe. Much of that renewed sense of self determination had been built on the idea of a powerful military capability underpinned by hope in the development of inter-Arab cooperation. But the result of the war was the decimation of the militaries of three powerful Arab states. In the aftermath of the war, foreign powers heaped praise on the performance of Israel's military and studied its tactics. In comparison, the Arab militaries, particularly Egypt, were shown to have been incompetent. Jordan had lost the West Bank and Jerusalem, Syria had lost the strategic Golan Heights and Egypt had lost the Gaza Strip and Sinai, which meant that it had lost two major sources of income, the Suez Canal and oil fields. The regime that had whipped up the Arab masses in the Gulf against their pro-Western royalty was forced to take aid from Kuwait and Saudi Arabia. Instead of liberating Palestinians, 1.2 million more were now subject to Israeli rule.

The defeat of 1967 was more than a catastrophe, which was the popular word used to describe 1948. The new Arab orders that had ridden into power on a promise of rebuilding national, and Arab honor, had been humbled, yet again. This time there was no room for excuses. The defeat – made all the more painful by state-controlled propaganda promising victory right up to the last minute – was felt on a personal level by millions. The defeat shook the masses' faith in the new left-wing, secular military governments that had promised so much but delivered so little.

For many Arabs who lived through the defeat of 1967, the iconic singer Umm Kulthum gave voice to the deep humiliation that went beyond the loss of blood and treasure. One of her songs, "El Atlal" ("The Traces"), evokes the dark days after the Arab world's worst defeat. A love song with lyrics such as "Give me my freedom, set free my hands so that I might give you everything, I will hold back nothing," moved listeners to tears. To this day, snatches of the tune are instantly recognizable to teenage Arabs and more than a few hardened Islamists have admitted to me they fight back tears when they catch a few bars of the song. Umm Kulthum sang the song in concerts across the Arab world and Europe and donated the proceeds to the empty Egyptian treasury.

Many across the Arab and Muslim world drew the lesson that the Arabs had lost to Israel because the Jewish state was built with its religious and cultural heritage very much in mind, while the Arabs had abandoned theirs in the belief European models would provide them with the economic and military strength they desperately sought. It wasn't only the Arabs who made this connection. On the other side of the political divide, the Israeli public came away from 1967 with a feeling that they were undertaking a divine mission, which strengthened support of the religious right and even seeped into the thinking of the predominantly secular left-wing Israelis.

In the Muslim world, the stage had been left vacant for Islamism.

As well as a change in the political consciousness following the war with Israel, Muslim nations, like other post-colonial developing states, were undergoing a shift in the makeup of their societies. The Western-trained elites who had inherited or wrested power from their former colonial maters were becoming increasingly marginalized. Improvements in public health without changes in social and cultural outlooks meant the population in poor urban and rural areas rocketed. And, at the same time, corruption and economic stagnation left this growing section of society without access to education, jobs or most other forms of social mobility.

Nasser himself had come from the growing class of people from humble beginnings but the social mobility that state-supported education and service within the government made possible didn't last long. Egypt, by the measure of other Muslim countries, did fairly well in promoting social mobility. The desire to overturn the existing order had been expressed in Egypt, Syria and Iraq by the new generation of army men and civil servants in leftist terms borrowed from the eastern side of the Iron curtain. But as the leftists became the new elites, and the heady days of Arab socialism passed, the politics of Islam became the new vocabulary of self expression. And, deriving from religion – or, according to its leaders, *being* Islam itself– Islamism had positions on personal, communal, national and international matters.

Iran's liberals were also agitating in the 1950s for a better deal from Western powers. Like Egypt and the Muslims of India, Iran also felt it had suffered humiliation at the hands of Western powers. It had never officially been a protectorate or colony but both Russia and Britain pushed forces into the country at will during the two world wars. Businessmen from the same European states maintained a choke hold over its economic development from the days the Qajar dynasty started granting concessions in the late 19th century. Even though Reza Khan had tried to build a nation on the rubble left by the Qajar shahs by bringing the local tribes under his control and centralizing the government, he could only operate in the margins of British and Russian power. Once the Second World War arrived on Iran's doorstep, he was forced to step down. Mohammed Reza, his son, ruled at the pleasure of the British government. After the war, the Anglo-Iranian Oil Company (AIOC), which was owned by the British government, practically ran a state within a state. It built and operated its own roads and airports, while negotiating its own treaties with the local tribes. Under the terms of the oil deal signed with Reza Khan in 1933, the company had full rights as to how much oil to pump and what price to sell it at. The Iranian government was only paid a small percentage of the revenues.

When the Iranian parliament, under nationalist politicians, seized its oil production in 1951, Britain and America imposed sanctions. The new prime minister, Mohammed Mosaddiq, tried to challenge the pro-Western monarchy's absolute grip on power and move it into a more ceremonial role. In 1953, the CIA engineered a coup to overthrow him.

Today, the threats to the West from the Muslim world come in the form of violent Islamists who kill civilians. But the first threats were not to Western lives, but to Western economic and political interests. And the leaders who personified those threats were liberals. Mossadiq was one of very few moderate liberals to take the reins of power in a modern Muslim state. Before him had come pragmatic leaders with ambitions for the immediate betterment of their nations. After him, opposition increasingly took the shape of Islamist rhetoric, which saw the entire Western-modeled government system as part of the problem.

Chapter 8

The Road to Radicalism

Nasser and the Arab socialists pushed Islam completely to the personal sphere of life and uprooted any of its traditional public functions beyond the ceremonial. The strand of thought that veered towards rejecting all Western influences, resulted in the ideology of Sayyid Qutb, the first ideologue of radical Islamist thought.

Qutb was born in an Egyptian village in 1906 and moved to Cairo in 1929. Unlike the traditional Islamic educational backgrounds of the revivalists of the previous generation, Qutb received a Western education. After finishing his studies in 1933, Qutb started work as a civil servant in the field of education. From 1948 to 1950, he undertook further studies in the United States.

A man of Qutb's background would have been expected to move towards the secular trend in the Muslim world. His education had been Western and he had lived in America. But, on his return, Qutb became deeply involved in the Muslim Brotherhood. In 1952, when Nasser overthrew the Egyptian monarchy, Qutb and the other Brotherhood leadership hoped the new president would enshrine their image of Islam in the running of the new state. At the time, the ideologies of Arab Socialism and Islamism were fluid and vague enough to make it seem possible the two could be combined into one government.

Nasser's early decisions not to ban alcohol or implement Islamic family and criminal law set the tone of what his new style of government would look like, and the Islamists were very much on the outside. The result was an assassination attempt on Nasser in 1954. The government used the incident as an excuse to move against the Brotherhood and arrested Qutb along with other leaders. Qutb spent 10 years in jail during which time he was tortured, before being released for a few months. He was then arrested again, tried for plotting to overthrow the state and executed in 1966.

Qutb wrote the books that form the basis of his ideological legacy during his time in prison. The first was a commentary called *In the Shade of the Quran*, while the other was his political manifesto, *Milestones*. Qutb's central argument is that the present world order is unjust because society is living by man-made laws and not God's laws. He called the state of chaos and injustice caused by the rule of man-made laws, Jahiliya, which is the term Islamic tradition gives to pre-Islamic Arabia. True freedom and justice can only be achieved through the imposition of Islamic law, he argued. And, the way to do that was to fight jihad.

The imposition of man-made laws robbed political communities of their freedom, Qutb explained, because the men who make the laws, the elites of the society, ensure that the system they create serves their greed for wealth while exploiting and oppressing the majority of the population. On an individual level, Qutb argued, mankind needed to submit to God's laws in order to attain a higher level of humanity and fulfill its destiny as God's rightly guided representative on earth. Ignoring God's injunctions left men and women concerned only with serving their base requirements for food, shelter and sex.

In Qutb's view, the forces of light (Islam) and darkness (Jahiliya) had been battling it out on earth since the dawn of humanity. He pointed to Western civilization as the source and epitome of Jahilya in the modern age. He argued that the Enlightenment replaced God with man in the Western world and promoted the view that man was nothing more than another sort of animal, which robbed society of a sense of belonging and promoted consumption as the new reason for existence.

Qutb's worldview placed Western civilization and Zionism in

the center of contemporary Jahiliya. And since Jahiliya sought to destroy any opposition to it, Western imperialism and Zionism were out to destroy Islam, the champion of those oppressed by man's tyranny over his fellow man.

It's often forgotten that the Islamist worldview seeks to refashion the world and replace oppression with freedom. The conceptualization of freedom is radically different to the one commonly understood in Western culture but at the core still lays the idea of improving the situation of mankind.

Like other totalitarian ideologues, Qutb imagines freeing people by force and acting unilaterally in the name of the masses because they have been blinded by a nefarious entity that wants to enslave them. The ideology shares with socialism and fascism the idea that ridding the world of a looming evil influence is the only way to attain ultimate freedom. Socialism sees that evil in class and fascism sees it as an outsider. Qutb's difference with these other two ideologies lies in who they identify as their enemy.

Qutb's position was radically different from the Islamic revivalists who came before him. Where they tried to find what the Islamic world could learn from Western civilization, Qutb rejected it altogether. His ideas appealed to those from poor backgrounds who found that Western education was not the key to advancement that they had hoped. These were the people who had suffered for two generations. Modernity had not kept its promise of prosperity and social justice. Instead, they found themselves increasingly at the mercy of corrupt officials and losing out to foreign businessmen who were often operating in their countries with the dispensation of their own rulers. The urban middle class was also feeling the humiliation of Western dominance, but it was also reaping some of the rewards of wealth and status. The mass of the population was getting nothing and losing a lot.

Qutb's depiction of the West as a source of evil, rather than a society to be envied and copied, made perfect sense to the majority of the Muslim world who saw little good coming from the West. The idea that Muslims had a way of life that was superior to the colonizers played well to a collective sense of wounded pride. At the same time, Qutb was also offering answers that didn't involve having to admit the Western world was in anyway superior to Islam.

The underlying frustration and anger that fuelled Qutb's thinking was also being felt in Pakistan, the Muslim nation carved out of British-run India as a homeland for the subcontinent's Muslims. One Pakistani thinker had a profound impact on Islamist ideology, and his thoughts are still a subject of common debate amongst students in the Arab world.

Mawlana Mawdudi developed an ideology that allowed Islamist thinking to adapt to the new nation states that traditional scholars had considered irreligious. Mawdudi saw the traditional Islamic scholars of Muslim India, and so inherited by Pakistan, as British collaborators since the fall of the Delhi Sultanate in 1857. As opposed to the Brotherhood in the Arab world, Mawdudi wanted "top down" transformation of Muslim society. Like Qutb, he saw the strict adherence to Islamic law as the cure-all for the problems of the Muslim world. But unlike Qutb, he concluded that right-thinking Muslims should work in the open and form political parties and aim to seize power. The party he founded was called Jamat-e-Islami and exists to this day. Its supporters mainly come from Pakistan's middle classes and even if they aren't personally religious, its followers exhibit a deep attachment to Mawdudi's idea that Muslim nation states have no place in the world and should be replaced by one powerful Islamic state. Mawdudi did not, of course, first voice this idea. Rather, he gave ideological solidity to a vague but deeply held political aspiration.

It was Mawdudi who influenced Qutb after his work had been translated into Arabic from Urdu. The Egyptian had taken it one step further by committing his vanguard of adherents to overturn the state instead of working within the structures of the state.

In the end, neither Qutb or Mawdudi was successful. The governments of Pakistan and Egypt, two of the world's largest Muslim countries, have not fallen to Islamists. Not yet, anyway. Their failure was their inability to find a place for young unemployed men in their plans for a new world order. Islamist politics, however, did succeed in capturing power in Iran. The reason was simply that Iranian Islamists connected with the growing ranks of impoverished and dispossessed young men and women who had enough education to be politically aware but not enough family influence to gain employment.

After regaining his throne with the help of a CIA planned countercoup that removed Mossadiq from power, the Shah became even more reliant on the Western powers than his father had ever been. His rule became synonymous with political repression and violence. Ayatollah Khomeini was at first one of a number of political figures denouncing the shah's pro-Western, autocratic government. But he was also the first political Islamist ideologue to come from the clerical classes – and in Iran the Shi'ite clerical classes were much more structured, hierarchical and independent than in Sunni Egypt and Pakistan, where Islamist thinkers found themselves in theological conflict with the scholars. But like the Islamists of Pakistan, he framed his opposition to the ruling elite around their perceived Western habits and policies. In Egypt, Nasser had carried out policies that were designed to challenge Western control of Egypt's resources so the Islamist criticism of his secular government had limited impact. But in general, Islamist opposition to secular rulers was framed around their progressive policies because these were seen as synonymous with Western foreign policy.

Chapter 9

Rise of the Radicals

During the 1980s and 1990s, the Muslim world made fleeting impressions on Western consciousness through news about reactions to Salman Rusdie's novel *The Satanic Verses,* or massacres in Bosnia and conflict in the Palestinian territories and Chechnya. For a generation of young Muslims, these events helped to forge the Muslim outlook that would react to the 9/11 attacks at the start of the new millennium.

I arrived in Egypt to take up my first journalism job in the summer of 2000, after graduating the year before. The Palestinian second Intifada (or uprising) had begun shortly after Ariel Sharon decided to take a highly provocative walk on the site of the al-Aqsa mosque in Jerusalem, Islam's third holiest site and the focal point of grief throughout the Muslim world. To Palestinians, Muslims and many others, Sharon's visit signified his intention to eventually tear down the Islamic monuments on the site and rebuild the ancient Temple of Solomon, which is thought to have stood on the same site before the Romans destroyed it in 70AD as punishment for the Great Jewish Rebellion against their rule.

Sharon's visit sparked riots and the Israeli police responded by shooting and killing Palestinian and Israeli Arab demonstrators. In the first five days after Sharon's visit, 47 Palestinians were killed and 1,885 wounded while 70 Israeli police were wounded and at least one killed. In October, two Israeli reservist soldiers were lynched in the Palestinian Authority-controlled city of Ramallah. The tit-for-tat violence continued until the Palestinians, who were coming off worse, began resorting to suicide bombers in the summer of 2001.

Years later in Britain, I met young British Muslims who had been watching these events on their television screens. Abdur Rahman and 10 of his friends, who spend nearly every day preaching from a street stall in Luton, were angry in their tone and extreme in their approach – they do not mix with non-Muslims, live off state handouts and spend a lot of time demanding the deaths of those they feel are insulting Islam. In their view, a legitimate Muslim government would force the observation of these rules. Of course, they didn't see themselves as extremists, they saw themselves as "proper" Muslims who "follow the religion as it was meant by God to be followed".

But Abdur Rahman's beliefs didn't appear out of nowhere. He didn't suddenly hit some Islamic form of puberty. Abdur Rahman clearly remembers the moment when he decided to break with the conformist middle-class aspirations of his Bangladeshi immigrant family and join the fraternity of what some British commentators have called "the terror state within".

"I watched the Israelis kill Mohammed al-Durrah on TV," he said as his cloaked and bearded friends nodded. "I told my mum, 'I feel like that is my brother they have killed'. I couldn't stop crying."

The death of Mohammed al-Durrah made headlines in the West for a few days as Palestinians and Israelis argued about who fired the fatal bullet. Within a week, his death faded from view. But in the Muslim world, high streets have been renamed after the 12-year-old Palestinian who was seen in news footage screaming in fear and clutching his father before being shot and killed by what turned out to be Israeli bullets.

Abdur Rahman and his friends noticed British leaders, who said they represented them, had not expressed the rage they felt. The general response in Britain had been to blame both sides for the violence. The young men from Luton felt young Mohammed al-Durrah's death was easily forgotten by the West because he was "just another Muslim". And as Muslims, even, at the time, non-practicing ones, they identified with the Palestinian child's life, and his death. Seeing Mohammed al-Durrah die on television made Abdur Rahman find out more about conflicts within the Muslim world. The more Abdur Rahman later found out about the oppression of Muslims in Kashmir, Chechnya and by Western-friendly Muslim regimes in countries like Egypt and Algeria, the more his anger grew. And when he looked around and noticed that the issues burning away in his newly developing political consciousness were of little concern to Britain, the less he felt he belonged.

Abdur Rahman and his friends chose to snatch back their self-respect by rejecting in every way possible the source of their humiliation – the West. As a result, they believe it is part of their religion to wear robes when British men wear trousers; they grow beards that they never trim when the norm is to be clean shaven. They think they must take four wives when Islamic tradition sees polygamy as an option not a duty. They reject banking, insurance and every other mundane facet of everyday existence in Britain. The basic idea is rebellion sanctified by God and it helps them feel as if they have scored a victory against the system they see as responsible for the misery – past and present – of their brothers and sisters in Islam.

Throughout the 80s and 90s, death and destruction in Bosnia, Chechnya and Kashmir made it on to the news more frequently, while Israel was seen as killing Palestinians and invading and bombing Lebanon. At the same time, Muslims states seemed to collaborate in the first U.S.-led war against Iraq against the will of their populations. After the war, Iraqis suffered a decade of sanctions. For more than 25 years, the Muslim world's resentment against the West and Western aligned leaders grew steadily. In Europe and North America, policy makers and public opinion realized that hostile states like Iran and Syria were antagonistic towards the actions of their countries. But what they didn't realize was that popular resentment was even greater in countries like Egypt, Bahrain and Saudi Arabia, where the ruling class had deep ties to Britain and the United States.

I heard airplanes had crashed into buildings in New York when I was stepping out of the campus of the American University in Cairo. I had been meeting the public relations department about writing an article on the warm reception American students felt they received from the residents of the Arab world's largest city. At the main gate, I stopped by the security guard's cubicle and saw a television set inside tuned in to the repeated footage of the two planes flying into the World Trade Towers.

I spoke to my editor at the Middle East Times and decided to get working on a story on Arab reaction to the still unfolding events. The city was in a state of confusion. No one knew who exactly had attacked America or whether the incidents had been part of a tragic accident. Later in the day, news emerged that another airliner had crashed into the Pentagon and one had ploughed into a field on its way to hit the White House. The streets were strangely quiet in a 24-hour city that is famed for never sleeping. Word had spread around that the government had banned any sort of public gathering.

I spent the evening striking up conversations in the glitzy cafés of Cairo's upper income districts and the sawdust-strewn speakeasies in the Imbaba district, where the authorities had faced a rebellion by Islamist militants only five years before. In the first hours after the attacks, people's opinions were still fluid and changing according to every new piece of information or rumor they heard. And even though the attack had taken place at a time when American policy was at its most unpopular, the reactions of Egyptians were by no means predictable. In the Mohandeseen district, teenagers who spoke Arabic second to MTV English and wore nothing but foreign brands, pumped their fists in the air every time the looped television footage showed the World Trade Towers collapsing. To explain the scene to a Western audience, I had to ask them how they reconciled their obvious Western cultural leanings with their glee at seeing the institutions of that culture collapse and burn. I was embarrassed asking the question as I knew the answer. "Culture and policies are different," was the sentence I heard time after time.

In Cairo's central bazaar in the old city, I talked to a man who sold copies of the Quran and intricately carved wooden book rests. He served tourists while keeping half an eye on the television playing in the corner of his shop. I asked him what he thought of the attacks and who he thought was responsible. He replied; "People are saying some Muslims are involved. That could be the case. But if Muslims did this, I want to ask them if this is a way to express your anger? Innocent people who work to pay their bills and send their children to school died there. And how many of them were poor immigrants; people from countries that have nothing to do with American policy here. And, how many were Muslims?"

The following day, Egyptian television started playing close up footage of people jumping to their deaths from the burning towers. Walking and driving through the immensely crowded central Downtown area of the city, I saw the footage playing on hundreds of television sets to scores of people crowded around each one. When I took my place in one of the cafés in front of one of the screens, I noticed nearly everyone, from the most hardened left-wing activists, to young activists of the Brotherhood, were transfixed by the images on the screen shaking their heads in disbelief and shock at the sight of ordinary people making the choice between being burned alive or falling to their deaths. A day later, the U.S. embassy in Cairo opened up a book of condolences. For one of the very few moments in recent history, rich and poor Egyptians stood in the same queues with no one earning a ride to the front on the basis of their social standing or wealth. They all stood for hours in a hushed line snaking around the American embassy waiting to express their common humanity with the men and women they had seen leaping from the towers. In the first few days after the attacks, Cairo's residents showed that although they cheered the destruction of symbols of Western power, they could not bring themselves to cheer the deaths of ordinary office workers. But, that sentiment dissipated by the time the U.S. invaded Afghanistan. As U.S. and British warships crossed the Suez Canal, the sympathy had completely vanished.

The Al-Qaeda attacks on the United States were grounded in anger and the need for revenge. Osama bin Laden admitted as much in his public statements. In a speech broadcast in October 2004, Osama bin Laden said; "And as I was looking at those towers that were destroyed in Lebanon, it occurred to me that we have to punish the transgressor with the same". The situation bin Laden was referring to occurred during the 1982 Israeli invasion of its northern neighbor. According to him, America allowed Israel to invade and provided it with assistance. "We had to destroy the towers in America so that they taste what we tasted, and they stop killing our women and children," he went on in the same message.

However, any political ideology that takes its reference points from Islam has to be able to defend its positions theologically in front of the Muslim masses and religious scholars. If it can't make a strong case for its conformity with Islamic values, it will lack legitimacy. Al-Qaeda marked a new direction in the ideology of resistance that had developed from Syed Qutub's teachings. To have a hope of gathering popular support, it needed to develop an ideological basis in Islam.

Montasser al-Zayat is an Egyptian lawyer who, as a young Islamist, was imprisoned with Ayman al-Zawahiri after the al-Qaeda ideologue was suspected of involvement in assassination of Egyptian president Anwar al-Sadat in 1981. Zayat explained Zawahiri's ideology to me in his office central Cairo.

Zawahiri decided that the focus of the military efforts of the

Islamist groups fighting to restore the power of the Muslim world should move from local regimes to Washington, which he saw as the main power center of a system that supported the local rulers. Zawahiri called the local regimes the "near enemy" and the "far enemy" referred to the governments of non-Muslim countries that sat on top of the current world order.

The near enemy didn't have to be regimes that were allies of the West. It included any state that used Western cultural and institutional norms to find an accommodation with the West. That accommodation could mean that they had a strong alliance with the West, such as Egypt, or that they merely tried to avoid invasion, as in the case of Iran or Syria. But either way, in Zawahiri's view, by failing to implement the Islamic Sharia law in full, in the Ibn Taymiyyah mold, the rulers of these countries were prostrating themselves to the West's interests to preserve their own positions while selling short the aspirations of the Muslim masses.

Zayat thinks that both Zawahiri and Osama bin Laden believed the key to success lay in taking the fight directly to America instead of attacking its satellites. To this end, the two men also agreed that they should employ a new tactic – targeting civilians. Islam expressly prohibits killing non-combatants. But the logic of civilian massacre had been gaining ground since it had been employed during the 1992-1997 Algerian civil war. The killing was wanton, but since the fighters doing the killing wore their Islam very prominently they needed an Islamic excuse for the massacres. So, again borrowing from Ibn Taymiyyah, they argued that the civilians, by not supporting Islamic law, had forsaken Islam. The process of declaring a Muslim's Islam void, essentially excommunicating them, is known as "takfeer". Those who practice it are known as takfeeris. It not clear whose idea it first was, accounts differ, but Bin Laden and Zawahiri expanded this concept and mixed it with the concept of the "far enemy" to justify killing Western civilians.

In February 1998, Bin Laden and Zawahiri announced their alliance and the formation of the International Islamic Front for Jihad on the Jews and Crusaders. Along with the announcement, Bin Laden issued a religious ruling, a fatwa (which many felt he was not qualified to do) calling for attacks against Americans anywhere in the world. His justification was that American civilians by their right to vote and through tax payments have made themselves responsible for the deaths of Muslim civilians, and for that reason they can be killed as combatants.

One strand of al-Afghani's ideology had completely failed. Taking on aspects of Western ideology had done nothing for the Muslim world. Socialism, capitalism and nationalism had all been tested and failed. In fact, political instability had increased and relative to other parts of the world, life in Muslim states was getting harder. The only way to go seemed to be to retrench further, to look deeper for the purest form of Islam. The ideology of al-Qaeda and the other takfeeri groups like it, offered that path. Imitating the West had failed, this new ideology offered the chance to completely reject every facet of the West.

In 2008, in a run-down café in southern Lebanon, I found some members of the new generation of young men drawn to this ideology. The young Arabs I met in 2003 on their way to defend Iraq looked more like computer technicians than warriors. They had little fixed ideological underpinnings beyond defending Muslim honor, lives and property from an invading army that they believed was bent on pillage. I had wondered then if Hisham would discuss Arab popstarlets on the frontlines as he had with me in Cairo. I couldn't imagine him working a rifle. The men sitting at the plastic table in front of me, on the other hand, I was sure knew how to work a rife – and probably much more. Men like Hisham either died in Iraq or have returned trained and battle-hardened.

To meet the two men, I took a bus from Beirut and arrived in Sidon less than an hour later. Outside the small bus station, a man found me and led me through nearby streets filled with semi-derelict shops selling cheap clothing until we reached a small café. The man in his early 40s who had led me on a fast 20-minute hike through town frisked me outside the entrance. I had promised not to bring any recording equipment and had been advised to leave my British passport in Beirut – just in case. At the far end, wearing a Palestinian keffiyeh loosely around his face, sat Haider. At least that's the name he used as we shook hands when he rose to greet me before we sat together at the table. The man who had accompanied me sat with us and used the longest sentence he had spoken in my presence to ask what I wanted to drink. When I answered, he ordered us all – in Lebanese-accented Arabic – a round of tea.

A little reluctantly, Haider said that he was something of a boffin. He was 24 years old and from Khamis Mushayt, a town in southern Saudi Arabia near the border with Yemen. He decided to fight in Iraq after becoming angered by his own government's apparent inability to influence American policy and its silence in the face of torture and mistreatment by the Americans. He had grown up hearing from the state media that Saudi Arabia's relationship with America gave it much influence over the super-power. Iraq had shown to him and many others, he said, that in reality their government had "surrendered" to preserve the ruling family's grip on power.

One of Haider's teachers on the Yemeni border had trained him to turn his interest in science into an asset for the mujahideen fighting against foreign occupation of Muslim lands. He had been in Iraq for 15 months – mainly based in the northern town of Mosul – helping to develop and build the IEDs that have claimed the lives of hundreds of US and British soldiers.

When Haider first entered Iraq through Syria, there had been about 2000 foreign fighters like himself inside the country. Now they were leaving and only about 150 remained. Most of the foreign fighters inside Iraq had always been Saudis and Yemenis, a few other nationalities such as Turks were also present, he said. The Saudis and Turks were mainly going to Afghanistan and the Yemenis to Yemen or Somalia, where al-Qaeda was keen to establish a presence.

Chapter 10

Bursting the Bubble

The invasion of Iraq initially was a gift for al-Qaeda. It gave the organization, battered by U.S. action in Afghanistan and international efforts to close down its funding, the chance to take on U.S. troops and show the Muslim world that it could succeed where every Muslim army for more than two centuries had failed.

All it had to do in Iraq, was show that the U.S. – the standard bearer of the West and the world's only superpower – could be challenged.

The day before the "shock and awe" campaign officially began, I was invited by an Egyptian journalist to have dinner in a journalists' club in Cairo. My friend, Khaled, worked for a left-wing opposition newspaper. We had known each other for a year and spent a lot of time arguing about the nature of Arab politics over endless cups of coffee. As a good Arab socialist my friend Khaled believed strong leadership and a one-party state were the right way to run an Arab country. His only problem with the current regime was that it wasn't sufficiently independent from America and therefore was too meek in the face of Israeli excesses against Palestinians. I argued that the problems he identified the result of having a one party state. I pointed out that Khaled was arguing for a government that would put dissenters in prison. And if someone with his outlook came to power, he – or she – would be no different than the current regime.

Khaled's friends from other newspapers joined in the discussion. Most were passionate, ideological and very badly paid journalists from opposition newspapers. The others were better paid, but more frustrated because they worked for state newspapers that were self-censored by the state-appointed editor.

Everyone opposed the coming invasion. But apart from the fear of loss of innocent life, they believed the invasion and subsequent occupation would, in effect, spiritually remove Iraq from the Arab world. They did not doubt that America would make Iraq prosperous, reform its educational system and end corruption and nepotism. As one of the men around the table, a journalist from the flagship state-run daily al Ahram, said, "The Americans will give them Western style lives and the Iraqis will forget about us and they won't care about Palestine."

The belief in America's competence was unquestioning and unshakeable. And, largely, I agreed with them. The tragedy for America in Iraq and Afghanistan wasn't only that the words "Guantanamo", "Abu Ghraib" and "Bagram" will be forever thought of as giant stains on America's claim to be a leading light in the world for human rights and the rule of law. The failure of America's mission to rebuild Iraq and Afghanistan have showed the Muslim world that America is not good at the very things that define it as a superpower: creating wealth and fighting wars.

An unpublished U.S. federal report into the rebuilding of Iraq obtained and published by the New York Times in December 2008 branded the enterprise a $117 billion failure beset by bureaucratic mismanagement and a lack of knowledge about Iraqi society. The report outlined how the American mission in Iraq actually infected Washington with the sort of poor governance that plagues the Middle East. The report is full of examples of how American officials broke their government's own rules, and still managed to do no more than bring Iraq the level of infrastructure in had in the last days of Saddam's rule.

Instead of fixing Iraq, the badly thought out mission in Iraq managed to damage America. One passage of the report points out that the secretary of state at the time, Colin Powell, accused the Pentagon of repeatedly and blatantly lying to other arms of government about how many Iraqi soldiers were finishing training.

In Iraqis' everyday lives, this sort of bad government has immediate effects. Corruption is rampant. A police job can be bought for $500, painkillers for cancer patients sell for $80 for a few capsules and nearly everything that passes through the government's hands is available for the right price.

The situation in Afghanistan is no better. Many Afghans thought America, the country that could put a man on the moon, would be able to bring them clean water, electricity and jobs. They were bitterly disappointed. America led the invasion of Afghanistan in 2001. Eight years later, you can buy the post of provincial police chief for $100,000. If you want to swing a judge your way you need about $25,000. To get a relative wrongly arrested by the police released, you need $4,000. And you have to give the police $6,000 for every truck you want to drive across the country if you don't want them to tell the Taliban that you are coming. From the lowliest traffic policeman to the family of the president, it seems every Afghan working for the American-backed government can be bought.

Afghans say their country has always suffered from corruption. But they have never before seen it on the scale it has now reached. Transparency International, a German organization that measures honesty in governments, says Afghanistan is the fourth most corrupt country in the world. Iraq is the third. Only Somalia and Myanmar are worse.

In Afghanistan, the Taliban have been gathering support by proving themselves to be an alternative to the corrupt Western backed government. Syed Saleem Shahzad, a Pakistani journalist with the Asian Times, travelled to areas of Afghanistan under Taliban control in 2006, when Iraq dominated the headlines in Britain and America. As he travelled to Gereshk in Helmand province by taxi, Shahzad saw that the Afghan police, the sole representative for many Afghans of the new Western-backed government, was not a popular institution.

> We passed through several official checkpoints, but the Afghan police didn't check anything, only demanding that the driver pay 10 Pakistani rupees.
>
> "This is not an octroi (toll). This is pure extortion by the police and we pay because we do not have any option," the driver muttered. The Afghan police do not have a good reputation among the masses. They are notorious for being involved in extortion, and they love to shake down strangers. They are not beyond kidnapping, and even assassination.

Musa Qala is a strategic town that has changed hands several times. A local told Shahzad that the inhabitants' dislike for the Afghan National Army and police made it easier for the Taliban to take the town.

> "Life was made miserable by the Afghan police and the ANA," Abdul Nabi said. "They extorted money, robberies were common and it was impossible to travel anywhere after dark without being looted. There were many incidents of abduction of small boys and even girls. The Afghan police and the army were behind the crimes."
>
> "The public reaction was natural and they stood up against them. But then US aircraft bombed the area and NATO forces and the ANA tried to suppress the uprising.
>
> "Finally, the Taliban took to the battlefield. The whole town was emptied and British troops and the Taliban dug in against each other ... The Taliban won and the foreigners left the area.
>
> The people of the town then returned to Musa Qala, but now, without the police and the army, peace prevails. Robberies have come to a halt. There are no cases of abduction, and not any cases of sodomy," said Abdul Nabi.

The United States gifted al Qaeda the opportunity to humble its soldiers in the eyes of the Muslim world while destroying, through its own actions, its reputation for good governance, efficiency and competence. Men, like Haider, who have fought the U.S. on the battlefields of Iraq and Afghanistan exude a confidence that the Muslim world has been trying to recapture for over two centuries. More than questions of ideology and ethics, al-Qaeda's recruitment efforts pin their message on ideas of pride.

The video *Baghdad Sniper* was designed to play to this very raw emotion. Arab governments have tried for 50 years to play up their military accomplishments and instill a sense of pride, but for all their resources, their output seems clichéd and unconvincing compared to *Baghdad Sniper*'s slick spin and real-world footage.

The voiceover makes the video's point very clear and the use of actual events gives it a credibility that Muslim governments are unable to achieve.

> Our snipers are superior to those in the U.S. Army. Our men have only minutes to stop, scope, shoot and retreat while American snipers always shoot from a safe place under American control. American snipers hit easy targets. You hardly ever hear that they killed a fighter. Our men only ever hit armed enemies.

The people scripting the short video play straight to the rawest of Muslim nerves. The narrator explains how the Iraqis are doing a better job than the Americans, the world's most powerful military. And they are acting with honor. The video goes on: "We began with the Iraqi Tobuk rifle left behind by the army of the former regime. Now, we use captured American rifles which we have developed further by improving their operation and silencers."

If there's one thing that the Muslim world knows America is good at, it's building things. In *Baghdad Sniper,* the insurgents are saying that they have bettered them even on that front. By taking on America and surviving, the young fighters who went to Iraq have shown the Muslim world that Western power is not invincible or irresistible.

Another factor in the demise of American power in the eyes of the Muslim world is outside of its control. The rise of China has dispelled notions that Western-style society, or even that Western temperament, were the missing ingredients in the search for power, and therefore dignity, in the modern world. On the streets of Cairo, Karachi and Saudi Arabia, the populations of key U.S. allies are gleefully awaiting its demise. As America's global financial dominance ebbs away, governments scramble to make sure they get on the right side of the world's emerging superpower. For Muslim governments this means they have an alternative to U.S. support which makes them unpopular by association.

China, the rising global power, is making its play for the loyalty of the governments, but also the people, of the Muslim world. Speaking at a Sino-Arab conference, Chinese President Hu Jintao thanked Arab leaders for their position on Taiwan and human rights before adding China "will as always support the just cause of the Arab states and people", a veiled reference to the Israeli-Arab dispute, in which the U.S. is seen as hopelessly biased towards the Jewish state. The ties are quickly deepening. Last year, China became Oman's largest trading partner. Bahrain, which hosts the U.S 5th Fleet, has opened talks with China to increase military cooperation. Perhaps the situation is best summed up by Sudan's oil minister, Ahmed al-Jaz, who said; "We picked an ally out of necessity. But we got lucky that the ally turned out to be reliable, and a future superpower."

Chapter 11

The Limits of Extremism

Islamist extremism is not sustainable on an individual or collective level. Whenever it has existed in the past, its popularity has rested on its promise to deal with a specific threat. Once people have to live according to the rules of extremists and find their societies damaged by their unrealistic ideals of "pure Islam", support for extremists falls away.

At the same time the Saudi Wahhabis were sacking the holy cities of Mecca and Medina in the 19th century, an Indian Muslim leader also preaching a form of Islam inspired by Ibn Taymiyyah took to the streets of India's main Muslim cities preaching jihad to restore Muslim rule to India.

In 1826, Syed Ahmed established a base in the tribal Pashtun areas of what is now Pakistan's Taliban country, from where he hoped his jihad would sweep the British out of India. The Pashtun tribesmen he gathered around him had little direct experience of British rule. Their primary concern was the Sikhs who had conquered the settled Pashtun areas and ruled in Peshawar.

Coming from the same ideological foundation, Syed Ahmed and the Saudi Wahhabis reacted in similar way to their circumstances. The Wahhabis massacred the scholars and sheikhs in Mecca and Medina and waged war on neighboring tribes after denouncing them as non-Muslims. After Syed Ahmed's first disastrous battle with the Sikhs, he tricked a former ally who had switched sides to come to peace talks and then had his throat slit. He justified the man's murder, saying that by switching sides he had committed apostasy and his death was a religious obligation.

In 1830, Sayed Ahmed's Pashtuns took Peshawar. The Pashtun

tribes allowed Syed Ahmed to levy taxes on them and rule according to his teachings. In two months, the customs of the Pashtuns came into conflict with the laws Sayed Ahmed tried to impose and the tribesmen threw him out. Hearing about the Pashtun disarray, the Sikhs sent an army into the area to recapture the territory and killed Syed Ahmed and a small group of his followers in a one-sided battle.

Sayed Ahmed and the Saudi Wahhabis found Muslims most willing to follow them when they saw an obvious danger from a foreign enemy. Their alliances came under the most intense strain when danger passed and they set about applying their interpretation of Sharia law on their fellow Muslims. This is still true today.

After humbling the U.S. in Iraq, the obstacle to mass popular support in the Muslim world was al-Qaeda's use of gratuitous violence. The group's Wahhabi ideology justified its assassinations and bombings against Iraq's Shi'ites majority and Sunnis who opposed them. That approach lost them support amongst ordinary Muslims and proved to be a strategic mistake.

In April 2008, al-Qaeda's second in command, Ayman al-Zawahiri asked members of the public to submit questions on the internet and then issued answers. The first two questions demand answers from Zawahiri for al-Qaeda attacks that resulted in the deaths of Muslims. "My reply," al-Zawahiri said, "is that we haven't killed the innocents, not in Baghdad, nor in Morocco, nor in Algeria, nor anywhere else. And if there is any innocent who was killed in the Mujahideen's operations, then it was either an unintentional error, or out of necessity as in cases of al-Tatarrus [The use of human shields by the enemy]."

In his answer to the other questions about civilian deaths in Algeria, Zawahiri says the reports of casualties were all lies drummed up by governments that were "selling their countries to America and its allies". The answers didn't seem to satisfy the concerns of Zawahiri's questioners.

Extremism also has a dynamic of its own. Before 9/11, recruiters from organizations linked to al-Qaeda were visible on streets, and in community centers and mosques all over the world. After its attacks on America and the resulting "War on Terror", al-Qaeda can no longer recruit so openly. But an image built on defiance of a superpower and the ability to strike fear across the Western world gives it a new audience amongst the disenfranchised and dispossessed who want the societies they are shut out of to feel their anger. Many of al-Qaeda's new audience is young, angry, criminalized and adhere to, or adopt, a form of Islam not even Osama bin Laden would recognize. They identify the path they want to follow, and the people in the mountains on the Pakistan-Afghanistan border have only the most marginal influence on their activities and ideology.

On a dark winter's evening in a takeaway in Kilburn I arranged to meet Tariq, the leader of a London gang. Tariq and his friends robbed from anyone they considered were carrying out un-Islamic activities in their area. This meant that they raided brothels and crack dens and beat up drug dealers. They used Islam to justify their actions and called their gang the Taliban Group. "We live by Islam's laws," Tariq explained. "We enjoin good and forbid evil" - the tenet of the takfiri ideology that al-Qaeda springs from. Tariq explained that he had been to prison seven times. His father was an Arab and his mother was English. Although he didn't mention it directly, he joked casually about the beatings and abuse he suffered growing up. Like the other members of his gang, Tariq found Islam in prison. His number two was also from a Muslim background. The other two were converts from black West Indian families.

Although Tariq and his friends said they carried out their activities because they wanted to be good Muslims, they did well out of their "raids". They didn't answer when I asked what they did with the money and drugs they took. But someone later mentioned "expenses" that needed to be covered.

I also met Khaled, a 15-year-old gang member from the same area. Khaled had been born abroad; he said Palestine, but I suspected he only told me that for the associated glamour. On a disused rooftop in Brixton, he mapped out the London street gang scene for me. The biggest gang in London, he said, was the south-London based PDC – which has been alternatively known as the Peel Dem Crew and Poverty Driven Children in the 10 years since they formed. Many PDC members became Muslim in prison but the gang didn't have a specific Muslim ethos. Then, about two years ago, the older members of PDC decided to form the more violent younger Muslim members into a separate gang called SMS, South Muslim Soldiers. Khaled himself was part of the West London Bloods, which was modeled on the LA gang scene. They took their orders from a gang called SOA, or Soldiers of Allah, who used them as foot soldiers in their fights with other gangs.

A confused young man, Khaled would talk about getting drunk on buses and stealing mobile telephones while constantly smoking weed and telling me how he looked forward to hiring prostitutes over the weekend. But at the same time, he was keen to latch on to the al-Qaeda narrative. He told me that there were more young Arabs, mainly Iraqis, joining the London street gangs. "We are a consequence of this country's actions," he told me. "We don't want to act this way but these people have to pay."

When I told him that Muslim scholars would not condone his actions, he said, "The scholars are sell-outs. They say whatever their governments want them to say. We have to regain our honor in all the lands we live in. It's between us and Allah."

Many millions of young Muslims in the West and in the Islamic world are caught between the world of al-Qaeda, which is focusing increasingly on violence as a means and end in itself, and the failure of traditional forms of Islam. The problem is more acute for young Muslims in the West who lack other Islamic reference points that their peers in the Muslim world can still obtain from wider society. In the past, many have latched on to the vague concept of Islamic power because it gives vent to the anger that stems from frustration and disillusionment, but the majority – at some point – begin to question the one dimensional approach to Islam that it advocates.

At his talk in London shortly after announcing his split from Hizb ut Tahrir, Quilliam Foundation director Maajid Nawaz told an audience of British Muslims why he no longer believed in Islamist politics.

> In prison, I had time to contemplate my ideology and discuss it with other prisoners.
>
> One of the things that shocked me was how exclusionary Islamist ideology became the further you followed its route. I knew one man in prison who would condemn everyone he came across as a **"kafir"**, unless they could prove their Islamist credentials to him. He basically lived in a world where he was the only true Muslim.

The practice of declaring Muslims to be outside the faith – or a "kafir" – is central to extremist ideology and is known as Takfeer. It gives angry young men and women a sense of righteousness and superiority. Followed to its logical conclusions, it becomes divisive and ends up being used to justify killing Muslim opponents and civilians. Face to face with the reality behind the rhetoric, Nawaz, like many other Muslims who had attached themselves to extremist ideology, began to question the ideology he had adopted to address his personal grievances.

> This is what I realized: Islam is a religion. This religion can cater for more than one political ideology. God did not reveal one political or economic system, he only laid out guidelines. So much of it is open to interpretation.
>
> I studied in prison. As an Islamist, I believed that sover-

> eignty is for God alone. But then I realized that sovereignty is a modern concept. And that anyone who says sovereignty is for God is saying he is God because he is saying that he has sole right to say what God thinks.
>
> Isn't it about time we realized that political ideas are not from scripture but drawn up according to our preferences.
>
> In terms of identity, I realized that the companions of the prophet called themselves by their ethnic titles. For example Salman al Farsi - Salman the Persian. So you can be Muslim and Pakistani, Muslim and Syrian or Muslim and British.
>
> We have to promote debate so Muslims can develop a social contract which allows us to replace dictators.
>
> Islamism has to take responsibility for the way it has contributed to radicalism. I believe that Islamism is a modern phenomenon that has been attached to Islam and is detrimental to Islam.
>
> Islamism is an ideology that believes sovereignty belongs to God and there is such a thing as an Islamic state. I don't think there is an Islamic state any more than there is an Islamic car.

Islamists have proved they are the most powerful political force in the Muslim world. But their claim to represent the masses cannot, in the new political environment, go unchallenged. Young Muslims are unwilling to believe what they are told by their governments. To the discomfort of static regimes unused to having to explain themselves, a new marketplace of ideas has developed and more and more people, particularly the young, are no longer satisfied with slogans. It's proof they are after.

Muslims, as a whole, don't have any more inclination towards dour, austere interpretations of life that outlaw music, television, dancing or laughter than any other group of people. But this sort of austerity and fanaticism becomes acceptable if it's presented as the recipe to Islamic rejuvenation. People in the Muslim world will support austere, violent takfeeri fighters because they are in confrontation with the West, not because they feel drawn to austere, violent takfeeri ideology.

In January 2006, after a grueling few days of work covering diplomatic efforts by the Egyptians to keep the different Palestinian factions from turning on each other, a handful of colleagues and I decided that we needed a night out in Cairo. On one of the main streets of downtown Cairo, a part of the ancient city built in continental European style during the early part of the 20th century, we found a small sign that read "Kaiser" hung by two heavy wooden doors.

Cairo's working class bars are as low profile from the outside as they are rowdy once you cross the threshold. Like the other drinking holes of its type, the Kaiser had been reclaimed by Cairo's working men. New expensive bars modeled on the latest trends in London and New York were opening up in other Cairo districts. But in the downtown area, what we called the "dodgy bars" had become the preserve of taxi drivers, doormen, shop keepers and middle-ranking off-duty policemen. The high ceilings, faded velvet curtains and advertising for long-forgotten brands of whiskey gave a hint of the sort of upper class Egyptian and foreign residents that Kaiser, and other bars like it dotted around the area, used to cater for. But once inside, the plates of boiled beans, the bottles of cheap local beer, strobe lighting and the DJ and singer belting out the anthems of the city's slums made it clear who the bar's present clientele were.

As the evening progressed and the crowd became rowdier, the singer started going from table to table pointing the microphone at various guests and asking their names and where they came from. The DJ would then turn up the music and the singer would recite a couple of impromptu rhyming lines praising the guest and his hometown. Sometimes, the guest would add which company he worked for, or his profession and the singer would include that in his public praise. The crowd would cheer and the guest would be expected to throw money towards the singer and the DJ.

When it came to the turn of our table, a Canadian colleague with Palestinian family background thought it would be fun to pretend to the singer that he was part of the visiting Palestinian Hamas delegation. When the singer announced this to the crowd, the bar went wild and my colleague was pulled to the dance floor to shimmy next to the smiling waitresses. The crowd thumped the tables and waved their bottles of beer in the air shouting "Hamas, Hamas". My colleague then got carried away, snatched the microphone from the singer and started shouting out the names of Palestinian towns and dead Hamas figures. The crowd shouted back louder in return. Until my colleague got a little too carried away and shouted out, "the Muslim Brotherhood!" The crowd suddenly went quiet.

Hamas and the Muslim Brotherhood are ideologically linked even though the Egyptian group has announced its readiness to be more flexible on issues of personal choice than Hamas. But the crowd in the Kaiser didn't like the idea of praising the Brotherhood. Hamas was fighting the good fight far away from their everyday concerns. The Brotherhood, on the other hand, might well one day exercise its power over Egypt, and chances are the Kaiser patrons would have to find a more Islamic way of spending their free time.

After a half a minute of near silence, where my colleague looked at the crowd, and the crowd looked back at him, he decided to save the situation by taking to the microphone again. With the eyes of near a hundred people on him, he held up the microphone and shouted: "Osama, Osama, Osama!" The crowd erupted in cheers and applause. For the next five minutes, grown men in Egyptian robes and turbans stumbled out of their seats into the isles and held bottles of beer on their heads while dancing to the rhythm of the singer's repeated chants of al-

Qaeda's leader's name.

The Brotherhood has a far more moderate and flexible ideology than that of al-Qaeda. But Osama bin Laden was a hero for taking on the West. And – even better – he was far away and unlikely to ever bring his ideology to Cairo. If al-Qaeda fighters had found us in Baghdad's version of the Kaiser, chances are we would have all been killed.

Al-Qaeda in Iraq, like austere takfeeri groups throughout history, first gathered support because of its stand against foreign power but then lost it when the immediate threat lessened and ordinary people had to live under their rules. The same pattern led to the downfall of Sayed Ahmed's warriors in India, Abd al-Wahhab's Bedouins and the Taliban's lack of popular support amongst the people of Afghanistan as U.S. troops invaded in 2001.

If the Muslim world finally managed to ignore the West and plotted its own course, what would the result look like? If there was no resentment to exploit, groups like al-Qaeda would not find any support. Already, the group is finding it difficult to maintain its support amongst the masses it was hoping to radicalize and lead.

So, if left to its own devices, what sort of ideologies are likely to spring up in the Muslim world?

There are many other currents rooted in Islam now appearing that challenge the most widely held Islamic beliefs. In the United States, Amina Wadud, a female black American Muslim scholar has defied tradition by leading men in congregational prayers. Al Fatiha Foundation in Washington is dedicated to gay, lesbian and transgender Muslims.

Also in the United States, a young Muslim called Michael Mohammed Knight wrote a novel called *The Taqwacores*, in which he mixed Islam and punk rock rebellion to express his own disaffection. The book became a cult success and American Muslims began creating the subculture than Knight had dreamed up. The young Muslims who have read the book talk about it expressing their frustration with their faith and their country. One of the novel's Muslim characters is a girl who plays guitar in a rock band while wearing a burkha and leading men and women in prayer. Other characters include a pothead and a drunk. Knight told the New York Times in an interview that he became a Muslim as a teenager after studying in a mosque in Pakistan. Later, he became disillusioned with the faith after learning about the sectarian battles that followed the death of the Prophet Mohammed. Knight stopped accepting what others were teaching him about Islam and decided to refashion his understanding around the Prophet Mohammed's call to ignore leaders, destroy petty deities and follow only God.

In Britain, since 9/11 and the 7/7 attacks on home soil, Muslims have started a long overdue internal dialogue with new ideas being debated and criticized and old ones discarded. One organization collects and publicizes Muslim events in weekly mass emails entitled Londonistan Islamic Events. An email might include debates on the existence of God, media workshops and talks on history, as well as seminars on traditional Islamic theology and Arabic classes.

Even within the most orthodox communities, groups are taking up differing positions on various points, like the use of violence or the interaction between Muslims and non-Muslims. The audience at any of these events includes the most obviously observant in traditional robes, city workers in neat trim beards, punk rock Muslim teenagers and the merely curious. Speakers include Saudi traditionalist scholars who follow Ibn Taymiyyah's ideology as well as revisionists and even well-known personalities like prominent businessmen and the mayor of London, Boris Johnson.

If the West wants to help the Muslim world join the global community, it has to understand that its grievances are legitimate and not just a misunderstanding that can be solved by spending money on an international public relations exercise. Imagining the world's billion Muslims are waiting to become a carbon copy of the West will only lead to more faulty decisions, wasted lives and money.

Chapter 12

Conclusion

Islamic civilization's fall from its place in the world had more to do with internal decline than outside plotting. However, the Western world was gaining in power as Muslim civilization was fading, which made its lands and resources a target for traders and adventurers from Europe. For more than two centuries, the Muslim world has seen its wealth dissipate along with its sense of place in the world.

The Muslim world sees its history with the West in terms of centuries, while Western policy makers and journalists see relations in terms of decades. From the time Napoleon landed in Alexandria in 1798 and occupied Egypt until the Americans invaded Afghanistan and Iraq after 9/11, occupations of Muslim land and unfavorable trade treaties were justified in the name of freedom. In the collective consciousness of the Muslim world, talk of freedom meant corruption, foreign control and repressive local leaders. The rhetoric of returning to Islam came to be seen as the only way to return to a time of power, dignity and respect.

Instead of seeing Islamism as an ideology akin to fascism or Nazism, the West needs to understand what lies behind its slogans and what underpins its popularity.

William Sieghart, the chairman of Forward Thinking, a conflict resolution agency, says the British and American governments' misunderstanding of Hamas led to death and destruction. He explains that the political party founded by Hamas, the Reform and Change party, won elections in the Palestinian Territories on a promise of ending corruption and improving government services. "Palestinians did not vote for Hamas because it was dedicated to the destruction of the state of Israel or because it had been responsible for waves of suicide bombings that had killed Israeli citizens. They voted for Hamas because they thought that Fatah, the party of the rejected government, had failed them," he said in an article published in the Times. Crucially, Sieghart points out, Fatah fell in the esteem of Palestinians because like countless other movements in the Muslim world over the past two centuries, they were forced into a compromise that didn't deliver any benefits to those they claimed to represent. After seeing that Palestinians lost out due to Fatah's compromise, Hamas refuses to recognize Israel's right to exist.

As veteran BBC Middle East correspondent Jeremy Bowen said: "they (Hamas) will be the latest heroes to those people across the Islamic world who have latched onto the ideology of resistance to Israel and its American allies, which has become one of the region's most potent ideas."

But in the new landscape after 9/11, Islamists can't hope to maintain popular support if their short-term aim is to make people live austere lives under the shadow of brutal laws. Some of the largest Islamist groups have realized this. In southern Lebanon, Hizbullah has not been able to enforce the kind of personal laws enacted in Iran as it needs to maintain popular support among the Shi'ite community of the country to survive. In Egypt, a member of one of the Brotherhood's prominent families says a new relationship with America is possible.

In an article posted on an online news site in September 2007, Ibrahim El Houdaiby, a rising star in the Brotherhood, argued America needed Islamists because continued support for despots would only increase popular resentment. "The current and next American administrations have one of two possible alternatives," he argued. "The first is to continue supporting a regime that complies with all their demands yet spreads embedded anti-Americanism on the domestic level, and suffer the possible consequences of that, which will be devastating to everyone. The second alternative is to support real democracy in Egypt, and realize that the outcome would be a government that would not necessarily serve America's short-term interests in the region. The outcome will be a government that pursues Egypt's interests, and manifests the people's will, yet does not fuel widespread inherent hostility towards the United States."

Houdaiby's comments about "embedded anti-Americanism" extend to the Western world in general, and are true not only for the Egyptian government but also many others with pro-Western regimes. The leaders of these governments owe their continued grip on power on Western support but they often play to popular anti-Western sentiments. Anti-Western rulers such as those in Syria and Iran justify a lack of representative government and human rights on the basis that they bring with them Western control.

Barack Obama says he wants to end this situation. In Cairo, in 2009, to wild applause and adulation he said the United States aims to build a new relationship with the Muslim world on mutual interest and respect.

In practical terms, the challenge for Western policy makers is to understand and engage with these discussions and recognize where Western policy itself has to change and accommodate alternate interests and viewpoints. The West has to recognize that change is inevitable and begin to talk to groups like the Brotherhood and Hizbullah, which represent a political trend that is massively popular across the Muslim world mainly because of the failure of Western orientated regimes in the past. At the same time, Islamist groups have also to change and realize that fixating on turning the clock back to the golden era of Islam by forcing public behavior to fit a narrow dress code is not enough to build stable societies.

Muslims will have to find their own answers to their societies' problems because Western countries will not be imposing their will on the Islamic world in the name for freedom any more.

After the mess in Iraq and Afghanistan, it's unlikely politicians in Washington, London or Brussels will want to carry out ambitious projects to try and change the Muslim world through war and occupation. More significantly, it's unlikely they will have the funds to do it.

The events set in motion since 9/11 changed perceptions within the Muslim world. No one can yet accurately predict what new ideologies and ideas will rise from the interplay of local grievances and international events among a fifth of the world's population. But it's clear that a new way of looking at politics and society is forming even though it's among small groups of people. The key change will be the ability of broader sections of society to accept or reject ideas on their own merits and not become fixated by their relationship to the West. So, for example, the place of women in Muslim societies has to be decided on what people in those societies are comfortable with instead of a blind opposition to Western culture.

The mechanisms of influence in the West and the Muslim world have changed since 9/11. Previously, officials in Western capitals decided when and how to use violence in the Muslim world. Today, men and women in slums and refugee camps have the capacity to bring death and destruction to centers of power many thousands of miles away. World leaders will not be able to set policy among themselves without paying serious consideration to how their actions will be viewed on street level in the Muslim world. The Kerry Lugar bill passed by the U.S. administration in 2009 is an admission of this new reality. The new law seeks to change America's relationship with Pakistan from a primarily military focus to engagement with civil society. The U.S. administration said the bill would provide money for hospitals, schools and civilian infrastructure while opponents in Pakistan said it allowed the U.S. undue influence over internal Pakistani affairs. The underlying fear was that the U.S. was trying to limit Pakistan's military capability as it sought to ultimately weaken the country's independence. The intense hostility to the bill within Pakistani society shows the depth of suspicion that needs to be addressed.

After the Pakistani army expelled Taliban fighters from Swat, local residents said they had been shocked and frightened by the blood lust of the warriors who took over their town and hung police officers from lampposts. Once central authority was restored, there were reports and video footage of local residents killing a Taliban commander who remained in the town. But as the Taliban bombing campaign across Pakistan continued, many people in the country found it hard to believe their countrymen could be responsible for such carnage. As the bombs claimed hundreds of lives a week, Pakistanis condemned the actions of the attackers but struggled to believe they were anything other than foot soldiers for America, India or Israel.

Towards the end of 2009, takfeeri violence was spreading to Somalia and Yemen while Muslim governments from Algeria to Pakistan were losing credibility due to bad governance and corruption. Formerly solid regimes in centralized states such as Egypt were looking more fragile than they had in two decades. But this does not mean that extremist takfeeri violence is destined to take over the Muslim world. Osama bin Laden has failed in his aim to spark a global war between Muslims and the West. The methods of the men who claim to fight for his ideology and the kind of world they want to create alienates most of the world's Muslims.

The question now is what sort of alternate visions for the future the new voices of the Muslim world will be able to offer and whether the West will be ready to join them in a new relationship.

Contemporary culture has eliminated both the concept of the public and the figure of the intellectual. Former public spaces – both physical and cultural – are now either derelict or colonized by advertising. A cretinous anti-intellectualism presides, cheerled by expensively educated hacks in the pay of multinational corporations who reassure their bored readers that there is no need to rouse themselves from their interpassive stupor. The informal censorship internalized and propagated by the cultural workers of late capitalism generates a banal conformity that the propaganda chiefs of Stalinism could only ever have dreamt of imposing. Zer0 Books knows that another kind of discourse – intellectual without being academic, popular without being populist – is not only possible: it is already flourishing, in the regions beyond the striplit malls of so-called mass media and the neurotically bureaucratic halls of the academy. Zer0 is committed to the idea of publishing as a making public of the intellectual. It is convinced that in the unthinking, blandly consensual culture in which we live, critical and engaged theoretical reflection is more important than ever before.